The Knightly Tales of Sir Gawain

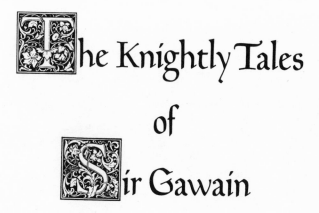

The Knightly Tales
of
Sir Gawain

with introductions and translations by

Louis B. Hall

Nelson-Hall Chicago

Manufactured in the United States of America

Library of Congress Cataloging in Publication Data
Main entry under title:

The Knightly tales of Sir Gawain.

   Bibliography: p.
   Includes index.
   CONTENTS: General introduction.—Sir Gawain and the
Carl of Carlisle.—The Green Knight. [etc.]
   1. English poetry—Middle English, 1100-1500—
Modernized versions. 2. Gawain—Romances. 1. Hall,
Louis Brewer.
PR1203.K65   821'.1   76-17866
ISBN 0-88229-350-8

Contents

General Introduction

The last half of the twentieth century is not an age of heroes. A hero seems to inspire an unquestioning belief so that the facts of his life are soon blended with legend: the legend that George Washington cut down the cherry tree and refused to tell a lie; the legend that Abraham Lincoln put the town bully in his place; the legend that Billy the Kid first killed defending his mother's honor. The hero attracts legends to such an extent that, as time passes, the deeds of his life do not diminish but expand.

This process of expansion is quickly checked in the twentieth century. The twentieth-century reading public demands that the legends of a man's life be separated from the facts. Then the facts that remain are subjected to the careful analysis of psychology and sociology. Accomplishments are attributed to the subject's overcoming psychological, sociological, or physiological weaknesses. Thus the myth of the hero cannot grow, for the story of his life is not planted in unquestioning belief.

The end of the Middle Ages—here primarily the late fifteenth and early sixteenth centuries—was an entirely different civilization from that of the twentieth century. The techniques we have today to separate fact

1

from fiction did not exist. The people who told the stories and the people who heard them then asked different questions from those to which psychology and sociology provide answers today. They asked what the hero did, not why he did it. His successes and failures, they said, were the result not of frustration but of fortune. And so, unlike the twentieth century, the Middle Ages was an age of heroes.

In fact, with the exception of the heroes of the Bible, never has an heroic tradition been preserved over so long a time or in so many countries as the chronicles, tales, and romances of King Arthur and the knights of the Round Table. This literature has endured from the sixth century until the twentieth, and it has spread throughout every country of the West. The stories of King Arthur circulated freely from storyteller to storyteller, and each time they were retold, they were adapted to new and special circumstances from medieval Paris to modern Broadway.

Within this great diffusion, the stories of Sir Gawain had their own birth, flowering, and fading. The process of adapting the Arthurian legend usually involved a storyteller's developing one of the knights of the Round Table into special prominence at the expense not only of King Arthur himself, but also of other knights already famous. In twelfth-century France, for example, Sir Lancelot received particular attention in such romances as Chrétien de Troyes' "Knight of the Cart," as well as in the anonymous, prose "Lancelot" part of the great vulgate cycle of the thirteenth century. In Germany the story of Perceval reached its zenith with Wolfram von Eschenbach's *Parzival*, though, of course, Chrétien left behind an unfinished *Perceval* which had six continuators.

In Britain, Sir Gawain had his most vital existence. Stories about Gawain first appear in the earliest collection of Arthurian tales, the *Mabinogion,* written in Welsh in the second half of the eleventh century. In the tale "Culwch and Olwen," Gawain, one of the warriors of Arthur's court, aids Culwch in winning Olwen, the daughter of Ysbaddaden, chief giant. In Welsh Gawain is called Gwalchmei, son of Gwyar, "because he never came home without the quest he had gone to seek. He was the best of walkers and the best of riders. He was Arthur's nephew, his sister's son, and his first cousin."[1]

In the first expansion of King Arthur's history, the legend of Arthur as world conqueror, Gawain occupies an important place as Arthur's greatest warrior. In this mythical history, King Arthur conquers those very people who, in fact, had conquered Britain: the Picts, the Scots, the Norse, the French, and the Romans. Among the chronicles Gawain's name appears earliest in William of Malmesbury's *Deeds of the Kings of Britain,* 1125:

> At that time [between 1066 and 1087] in a
> province of Wales called Ros [Pembrokeshire]
> the tomb of Walwen [Gawain] was found who,
> by no means unworthy of Arthur, was a nephew
> by his sister. He reigned in that part of Britain
> still called Walweitha [Galloway, Scotland], a
> soldier greatly celebrated for valor, but driven
> from the kingdom by the brother and nephew
> of Hengist, of whom I spoke in Book I, he made
> them pay severely for his exile.[2]

In Geoffrey of Monmouth's *History of the Kings of Britain,* 1136, we find the first details of Gawain's life. Geoffrey reports that Walgainus [Gawain] was the son of King Lot and Arthur's sister and that he was raised as a page of Pope Sulpicius. In Arthur's war against Lucius, Emperor of Rome, Gawain is one of three envoys whom Arthur sends to Lucius's camp. In this mission Gawain is no courteous diplomat. Angered by what the emperor's nephew says, Gawain chops off his head, invokes the curse of Cain on Lucius, and calls him a cuckold. In the war that follows, Gawain is the leader of Arthur's forces against the Romans and the greatest individual fighter. While this war is taking place on the continent, Modred at home takes over Arthur's throne. Gawain is killed in the final battle between Arthur and Modred.

The reputation of Gawain in Italy must have been favorable, however, for a figure of him appears in the architrave of the north portal in the cathedral of Modena, consecrated in 1184.

In the preface to the *Morte d'Arthur* of Sir Thomas Malory, 1485, William Caxton wrote that the skull of Sir Gawain could be viewed at Dover Castle, and there is little doubt that Gawain was popularly regarded as having had an historical existence. While the tales about him which survived vary widely, as we see in this collection, still three of his characteristics seem to be consistent until his reputation is overshadowed by that of Sir Lancelot: he was the most courageous, the most courteous, and the most amorous of the knights of the Round Table.

Gawain's reputation as the most courageous and best fighter can be observed in the tales of this collection. In "The Adventures at Tarn Wadling," he defeats Sir Galeron and in "Golagros and Gawain," he subdues Sir Golagros, both previously undefeated. No one else in these tales can match Gawain's prowess except Sir Brandles in "An Adventure of Sir Gawain."

Sir Gawain also achieved a reputation as the most courteous of Arthur's knights. After the late thirteenth century, courtesy become the hallmark of knighthood. Most knights are called courteous, as, for example, was Chaucer's knight in the "Prologue" to *The Canterbury*

Tales. In his article on Sir Gawain, B. J. Whiting concludes: "Among the traditional knights the leaders in courtesy are Arthur, Lancelot, Perceval and Ywain, and of these only Arthur can possibly be compared to Gawain in number and dispersion of references to the words courtesy, courteous, and courteously."[3] In many tales and in those collected here, Gawain's courtesy is contrasted with Kay's rudeness. Gawain is courteous even to the foal that belongs to the Carl of Carlisle, while Kay and Bishop Baldwin are not. In "Golagros and Gawain," the actions of Kay and Gawain again contrast as each tries to procure food at the first castle they encounter. Gawain's courtesy succeeds where Kay's boorishness fails.

Because he is a model of courtesy, Gawain, in early romances, is the favorite of Queen Guenevere, a role that is his in "The Adventures at Tarn Wadling" and "The Avowing of Arthur." His relationship with the Queen, unlike Sir Lancelot's, seems to have been platonic, but Gawain has an unrivaled reputation with other women as the greatest lover of the Round Table. Episodes that treat Gawain as lover are found most frequently in French literature. Many young women not only dream of being his lover but surrender quickly and willingly because of his reputation. In the French continuation of Chrétien's *Perceval,* which parallels "An Adventure of Sir Gawain," a girl whom Gawain meets in a wood surrenders as soon as she learns his identity. In another incident occurring in the prose "Lancelot," Gawain has learned that Floree loves him and stops at a castle to visit her. On the night of his arrival, while he is between wake and sleep, Floree comes into his room to see if he is warm or wants a drink. He kisses her, discovers she is cold, and invites her into his bed. This she refuses but suggests Gawain follow her to her own room. Here, as the story tells it, she loses her virginity and, discovering who her lover is, is overjoyed she has been the mistress of the best and most courteous knight in the world.

Although Gawain's reputation usually works in his favor, there are times when it does not. Once, when rumor has it Gawain is dead, he is kissing and embracing a girl when she starts to weep. She tells him that at fifteen she heard Gawain was unsurpassed in courtesy, handsomeness, and chivalry. She then resolved to yield herself to no one but him who now is dead. When Gawain tells her he is alive, well, and present, she refuses not only to believe him, but to give him even a farewell kiss. Later she comes to Arthur's court, believes what she sees, and goes to bed with Gawain without reservations.

As a lover himself, Gawain is usually on the side of lovers as well. The continuation of *Perceval* offers a parallel to "Golagros and Gawain." In the French version of the story, *Riche Soldoier*, the counterpart of Golagros persuades Gawain to feign defeat to save his honor in the eyes of his beloved and Gawain agrees. The motivation is political in the English version.

Gawain's reputation as a great lover must be understood when the Carl of Carlisle tempts Gawain with his wife then gives Gawain his daughter instead. By her remarks in the morning the reader knows Gawain has preserved his reputation. Their intimacy results in marriage, an ending unnecessary in most French stories. That the wife of Sir Bredbeddle loves Sir Gawain motivates the story of "The Green Knight," and Dame Ragnell's insistence she marry Gawain is especially dramatic in view of Gawain's history as a lover.

In "An Adventure of Sir Gawain," the fact that Sir Gawain does not defeat Sir Brandles, the only knight in this collection that he does not, seems to reflect a final change that took place in Sir Gawain's history, a deterioration of character. In later French romances, for example the *Suite de Merlin* (a sequel to an earlier life of Merlin), the prose "Lancelot," and the prose "Tristan," Gawain is pictured not as the best but as the worst knight in the world—cowardly, depraved, cruel, and treacherous.

Unfortunately, this late development influenced the three most popular of Arthurian chroniclers in English: Sir Thomas Malory of the late fifteenth century, Alfred, Lord Tennyson, of nineteenth century, and Edwin Arlington Robinson, of the twentieth. Malory does not offer a consistent characterization of Gawain, depending, as he does, on a wide variety of sources. However, in Malory Gawain is never the great warrior early storytellers showed him. He is defeated by Lancelot, Tristram, and his brother Gareth, and later he is rejected by his brother as treacherous and vengeful. Tennyson worsens Gawain's character over his sources by supplying psychological motives for his iniquities, and Tennyson, in general, finds him false, reckless, and irreverent. In the Robinson poems, as in Malory, there is no consistent characterization, but Gawain is forlornly ineligible to achieve the Grail, according to Robinson. In his *Lancelot*, Robinson used Gawain's anger at Lancelot's killing his brother to motivate many of his actions, but at Gawain's death, he redeems himself by forgiving Lancelot.

All the stories collected for *The Knightly Tales of Sir Gawain* were originally written in verse, but the verse narratives of Tennyson and Robinson, and all modern narrative, prose and verse, are meant to be read silently and alone. A minstrel, in contrast, sung these medieval tales or a storyteller recited them in the great hall of a castle, at pilgrim's inns, or possibly at a tavern. The minstrel might even have been a lord's daughter as occurs in "Sir Gawain and the Carl of Carlisle."

Probably the minstrel or storyteller himself did not compose the stories, no more than today a performer on television composes the songs he sings, the plays he acts, or the jokes he tells. These tales were transcribed by clerics, or at least by someone who could write. If the storyteller were illiterate, as happened many times, the tale could be read to him, and he memorized it quickly, still keeping the copy so his memory could be refreshed if he did not use the material over a long period of time. Professional storytellers who could neither read nor write, practiced in Ireland until well into the nineteenth century.

A modern printed story meant to be read in solitude and a tale meant for public performance have many differences in style. Half of these tales start with a command: "Listen, lordlings, for a little while," ("Sir Gawain and the Carl of Carlisle"); "Listen, when Arthur was king ("The Green Knight"); "Listen and hear the life of a great lord" ("The Wedding of Sir Gawain and Dame Ragnell"). The storyteller uses these tags to quiet the audience and get their attention. And the tale usually starts conventionally. Five of the tales begin with a hunt to allow time for the listener to adjust himself before the real action of the narrative is under way.

The relationship between the teller of tales and his audience is much closer than that between an author and his reading public. The teller uses "I" frequently, as we can observe, to protest the truth of what he is telling, to raise a picture "beyond description," or to make a transition from one character or one setting to another. In "Sir Gawain and the Carl of Carlisle," we find such phrases: "as we hear in the tales," "I can safely swear," or "I would reckon." At the beginning of "The Adventures at Tarn Wadling," the teller reminds his audience "as the book tells us," and at the beginning of "Golagros and Gawain," the teller says, "as honest men told me." After a lengthy description, many times the teller feels he can go no further. The dress of the Carl's wife is so attractive that the teller remarks: "I cannot begin to describe her clothes." When the Carl's daughter is dressed to accompany Gawain to Arthur's castle, the teller finds her so dazzling he says, "I could not even describe her." The teller finishes his description of the ghost at Tarn Wadling: "to describe this thing any further would tear out my tongue." The "inexpressible" is a traditional rhetorical device.

The tellers call attention to changes in place or character. In "The Avowing of Arthur," he says, "Let us first speak of the king, naturally," for it would be proper for them to take the highest ranking person first. In "The Green Knight," the teller moves from the court of King Arthur: "I am not going to talk about King Arthur any more right now but tell you about an adventurous knight who lived in the west country." Toward the end of "An Adventure of Sir Gawain," the teller tells his audience, "Now we leave Sir Gawain still sorrowful and we will speak more of Sir Brandles." The endings of the stories are usually carefully announced also, with the teller asking God's blessing on his audience, a way of thanking them for their attention.

All these techniques, that may appear artificial in print, are necessary when an audience must follow the oral narrative. In the intimate relationship that existed between teller and audience, the teller would know immediately if his story was being well received or if his audience was going back to their ale and wine. The storyteller had no reservations about taking a good story he had heard, using some of it, changing what he thought necessary, or perhaps even recalling it imperfectly. His interest had to be in pleasing his audience, either in twelfth-century France or fifteenth-century Scotland.

We can be certain that these stories appealed to fifteenth-century audiences or they would not have survived, but there is a fundamental difference between what they regarded as a good story and what we in the twentieth century regard as a good story. Sir Gawain or any of the other characters in the tales, with the possible exception of Dame Ragnell, are not distinct personalities like Joseph Conrad's Lord Jim, James Joyce's Leopold Bloom, or Saul Bellow's Arthur Sammler. Gawain manifests some or all of the aspects of his three characteristics, courtesy, courage or love. The fifteenth century is interested in how he demonstrates these even in the most difficult circumstances, his courtesy with the boorish Carl, his courage with a hideous ghost, his love with Lady Bredbeddle, or how, at the end of "Golagros and Gawain," he resolves the conflict between courtesy and his loyalty to King Arthur.

We must also be aware that the audience for the tales of Sir Gawain must have been young. It is estimated that in the fifteenth century between 40 to 50 percent of the population was under twenty. A man was a senior citizen at fifty. Sir Gawain may be seen as an expression of youthful aspirations, if we subscribe to the views of Erik Erikson in his essay, "Youth: Fidelity and Diversity." Physical courage in the context of violence, love at first sight and of short duration, courtesy and truth as a single-minded dedication to a person or a code, all these are youthful manifestations.

The audience for the tales was not only young, but, if we may judge from the provenance of the manuscripts, they might be located in a relatively small area of Britain. Four of them are in the fifteenth-century literary dialect of Scotland. All but two of them have their setting at Carlisle or in Inglewood Forest, not far away from Carlisle and at Tarn Wadling, a swampy lake within the forest.

Archaeological diggings in 1967 at the ancient hill fortress, South Cadbury, Somersetshire, unearthed pins, coins, and shards of the sixth century, and on the basis of this evidence, it has been suggested the fortress was Arthur's original Camelot. No such evidence nor even historical tradition has connected Arthur or Gawain with Carlisle and the Borderland between Scotland and England. Northern storytellers especially placed their stories at Carlisle, though in other versions of the same tales, the setting will be found elsewhere—Caerleon upon Usk, Wales, for example. Yet the stories of Sir Gawain must have had special appeal to the people of Carlisle and the Borderland to encourage a particular emergence of them in the late fifteenth century.

Carlisle was in the pathway of fighting from Roman times, and in spite of a treaty between Edward IV of England and James III of Scotland and in spite of truces and treaties between Henry VII of England and James IV of Scotland, there were raids and counterraids across the border and skirmishes in eastern Scotland. The Borderland, however, was relatively quiet, and although Henry VII was worried about James IV's amorous reputation, he finally allowed his daughter, Margaret Tudor, to marry James. Before Margaret arrived in Scotland, James rid his castle of his mistress and a brood of illegitimate children. James and his court, at least, would seem to have been more sympathetic toward Gawain as knightly lover than Tennyson was in a later era. Both Henry and James named their eldest son Arthur, and Gawain was always a popular given name in Scotland. Of course, legend associated Gawain with Galloway, as we saw in William of Malmesbury.

In his courage and his courtesy, Sir Gawain illustrated aspects of a moral code that was being advocated for knights and gentlemen during this transitional pe-

riod between the Middle Ages and the Renaissance.
The code had evolved gradually at least from the eleventh century, if not before, as an ethic separate from
that of the Church. It was not an ethic that would lead
to Heavenly bliss but one that would make the world an
easier and safer place in which to live. Courtesy, as it
can be observed in the actions of Sir Gawain, is rather
amorphous. Still it was important. The most important
virtue of the knightly code, however, was "truth," but
in these tales truth is more than speaking the truth, it
is a way of action. By truth is meant that a knight must
be true to his lord and true to his word. In "The Green
Knight," Kay volunteers to accept the challenge of the
Green Knight, but Arthur refuses him knowing his
word cannot be relied upon. Gawain's promises, by
contrast, are always kept. "The Avowing of Arthur" is
organized around vows that are kept. The mysterious
conduct of the Carl of Carlisle is explained by a cruel
vow he made, regretted, but observed for twenty years.

The code required that a knight be a great fighter,
and, as we have seen, Gawain was traditionally the
greatest fighter of the Round Table. What is pictured in
these tales, however, is not warfare but the joust, the
toughest contact, rather collision, sport in history. But
the joust of the tales is not even the joust as James IV
saw it in celebrations for his marriage to Margaret Tudor. Jousts are fights between two knights, not tourna-
ments, free-for-alls, among many. The two knights ride
at each other, cradling their spears which splinter
against the opponent's shield. If the knights are un-
horsed, then they fight on foot with swords.

By the sixteenth century, the armor used for jousts
was fifty pounds of plate steel that made the knight an
almost impregnable human tank. Other controls were
introduced to eliminate bloodshed and death.

In these tales, by contrast, the fights are bloody and

deadly. Gawain is wounded three times. At Golagros' castle, one knight is killed, two die of heart attacks, and both Gawain and Golagros are bloodied. Neither knight is using sixteenth-century armor but rather the armor of about a hundred years before, the armor of the battles of Crécy, 1346, and of Poitiers, 1356, a combination of plate and mail, not plate alone. In the fights with both Sir Galeron in "The Adventures at Tarn Wadling" and with Golagros, Gawain is wounded when links of mail in his neck piece, his pisan, are shattered. In the best steel plate, a gorget had taken the place of the mail neckpiece.

The armor that Gawain wore in these tales was an archaic idealization. In the battles that had taken place between the last half of the fourteenth century and the last of the fifteenth the importance of the knight in battle had vanished for all practical purposes. At Crécy and at Poitiers the English had defeated the French armored and mounted knights with their longbow. By the end of the fifteenth and the beginning of the sixteenth centuries the battles were decided mainly by infantry armed not only with longbows but also with bills and pikes, steel-pointed shafts sometimes as long as eighteen feet, that could be massed like bristles against cavalry. And the infantry was supported by even a more deadly weapon, the cannon.

These tales provided the people of Carlisle and of the Borderland with the dream world of Arthurian history. Arthur, Gawain, and the knights fight as they did a hundred years before; they hunt the largest deer, the most fierce boar. In armor covered with jewels, Gawain fights only unvanquished knights. The women are beautiful and loving. Even Dame Ragnell, the ugliest woman in the world, dresses in the best of silks and furs.

But this is a dream world on the edge of disaster. Five years after "Golagros and Gawain," September 9,

1513, the English and the Scots met on Flodden Field. James IV died at the head of his troops. His lords and 10,000 Scots died with him. For both sides the era of jousts and courtesy had passed. For both, though, Sir Gawain left a legacy of courage, courtesy, and love.

In modernizing the dialects of the tales I have tried to keep the language simple and straightforward, at one extreme avoiding something too modern and at the other something too archaic. The tales first were presented in an up-to-date language vital to those who heard them, and the language should remain so for us.

Rendering them from poetry to prose has been a natural step in modernization. The Scottish alliterative verse is elaborate and mannered, and any attempt to reproduce it in modern English, where the elaborate and mannered no longer seems to have a place, would give the tales a false and artificial timber that they really would not have had in the fifteenth century. At least the mannerisms would not have seemed artificial to that audience.

In addition the position of prose and poetry between our time and that of the tales has been reversed. Today poetry makes a statement of a personal or universal truth. In the fifteenth century such a statement would have been made in prose, probably Latin prose. Today, histories, texts, and stories are in prose. In the fifteenth century they were in poetry. Thus we have transferred the tales from their medium in the fifteenth century to their medium in the twentieth. The introductions attempt to illuminate some of the fundamental differences between the civilization of the fifteenth century and that of the twentieth century. Hopefully the introductions will increase the enjoyment and enthusiasm of the modern audience for the medieval tale.

ir Gawain

and

The Carl of Carlisle

Introduction

"Sir Gawain and the Carl of Carlisle" is both an excellent medieval tale and an effective modern short story. The listener of the fifteenth century and the reader of the twentieth alike become involved in the action, because whichever storyteller or cleric polished the tale into its present form was a talented artist.

The first paragraph introduces the main characters, all well known to the audience: Sir Gawain, Sir Kay, and Bishop Baldwin. It also puts them into a recognizable setting, Wales, and engages them in a familiar pastime, hunting, and in a common predicament, getting lost. The audience is involved immediately and anticipates the difficulties the knights will face when the only lodg-

17

ing they can find is in the castle of the infamous Carl of Carlisle.

The word "carl" was borrowed by the Scots and English from Old Norse, the language spoken by the Norsemen who settled in Northern Britain and to whom the word *karl* meant 'man." The English, however, made the word derogatory, and in Chaucer's *Canterbury Tales* it is associated with "churl"; in other works of the Middle Ages, it had a supernatural connotation.

All these meanings help explain the Carl of Carlisle as a churl with supernatural characteristics. He is a giant, but his size, two yards across the shoulders and nine yards tall, is not supposed to be mathematically accurate, but emotionally accurate, as are most numbers expressed in medieval tales.

The Carl of Carlisle is also under a supernatural spell. His power over his "whelps" and his reading the thoughts of Sir Kay and Sir Gawain reveal this. A shorter version of this same tale makes the curse explicit, but in the version used for this modernization, the spell is explained as a vow. The Carl is released from his vow when Gawain obeys him absolutely. The Carl, now changed, builds the abbey to atone for what he did while he was cursed.

This is one of the tales in which Sir Kay is contrasted with Sir Gawain. Good use is made of this contrast in building suspense as to what will happen to Sir Gawain after Sir Kay and the Bishop are knocked out in the stable. Sir Gawain passes his test by being kind even to a small horse. Kindness to animals was rare in the Middle Ages as reflected in its literature, though horses during those times had an honored place, especially for knights. Sir Gawain mourns the death of his horse, Grisselle, in "The Adventures at Tarn Wadling," and a knight without his horse was almost no knight at all, a point emphasized in "An Adventure of Sir Gawain."

In "Culhwch and Olwen" of the *Mabinogion,* not only does Cei (Welsh spelling of Kay) occupy a more important position than Gwalchmei (Gawain), but he is one of the most interesting members of Arthur's court:

> Cei had this peculiarity, nine nights and nine days his breath lasted under water, nine nights and nine days would he be without sleep. A wound from Cei's sword no physician might heal. A wondrous gift had Cei: when it pleased him he would be as tall as the tallest tree in the forest. Another peculiarity had he: when the rain was heaviest, a handbreath before his hand and another behind his hand what would be in his hand would be dry, by reason of the greatness of his heat; and when the cold was hardest on his comrades, that would be to them kindling to light a fire.[1]

These peculiarities did not survive into French literature, unfortunately. We find the rivalry that contrasted Kay and Gawain, to the detriment of Kay, started early. Chrétien de Troyes' *Erec and Enide* of the twelfth century is one of the earliest. A Dutch romance of the fourteenth century, *Walewein ende Keye* is organized on the theme of the contrast. The tales that make use of the contrast in this collection are "The Green Knight," "The Avowing of Arthur," "Golagros and Gawain." It is also featured in the comic romance "Sir Perceval of Galles."

Bishop Baldwin makes his only appearance in this collection in this tale. Although a Sir Baldwin of Britain appears in "The Avowing of Arthur," he is a different person. Like the names of Gawain and Kay, Bishop Baldwin's can be traced to the *Mabinogion.* In Welsh he is Bishop Bidwini, "Who blessed meat and drink."[2]

"Sir Gawain and the Carl of Carlisle" was modernized from the earlier of the two versions, the original found in a manuscript in the National Library of Wales, Porkington 10. Professor Robert Ackerman of Stanford University dates the handwriting of this version as about 1460–70. The first stanza of the original follows.

Lystennyth, lordyngys, a lyttyll stonde
Of on þt was sekor and sounde
and douȝgty in his dede.
He was as meke as mayde in bour
And þer-to styfe in euyry stour
Was non so douȝtty in dede.
Dedys of armys wtt-out lese,
Seche he wolde in war & pees
In mony a stronge lede.
Sertaynly wtt-outtyn fabull,
He was wtt arttyr at þe rounde tabull,
In romans as we reede.

The Tale

Listen, lordlings, for a little time, and I will tell you about a man who was steady and true, daring in his actions, humble as a maiden in her bower, but still fierce whenever he fought, no one so bold in his feats. It is no lie that he sought for deeds of valor both in warring and in jousting in many a foreign land, and certainly it is no fiction that he was with Arthur at the Round Table, as we read in the tales.

His name was Sir Gawain, and he won great honor also on the Isle of Britain. Scotland and England together are called the Isle of Britain in all true accounts, and Wales is a corner of that island. It was at Cardiff, Wales, that the King had stopped for a while with many of his noble knights who wished to go to England to hunt, as all great and stalwart lords are wont to do together.

"Let us first have mass," King Arthur said to his lords. "Bishop Baldwin shall say it, and then we will go to the forest for this is the time when deer are fat and we barons should hunt them."

Glad was Sir Lancelot du Lake; so was Sir Perceval, I understand, and Lanval, Sir Ewein the White Hand, too, and Sir Lot of Lothian, hardy and keen, Sir Gaudifeir and Galeron, Sir Constantine and Sir Raynbrown, the knight of the green shield. Sir Gawain was stewart of the hall. He was master of them all and prepared them for the hunt.

The King's uncle, Sir Modred, was there, a leader of noble knights, as people heard in the romances. Sir Engelyn, the noble knight, leading the fierce hounds who could do their job well. Sir Libeaus Desconus was there with proud nobles of all ranks; they would make the brown deer bleed. Sir Petypase of Winchelsea, a chivalrous fighter and rugged in the saddle. Sir Grandoynes and Sir Fair Unknown joyfully hallooed after the hounds. Sir Brandelys and Ironside, many brawny warriors rode that day on mounts sleek and swift.

Sir Ironside, I believe, was father of the knight with the green shield by a bonny lady, the fair maid of Blanche Land, in the manor of that beauty. Ironside was armed both in the heat of the summer and in the winter, always in combat with giants. His horse was Sorrel-Hand. His weapons and armor were the best, his shield azure with a griffin and fleur-de-lis; his crest, a lion of gold.

He was better at war and hunting than any king who was there and often bested the dragon and the terrifying wild bull. Great barons owed him allegiance. A more rugged knight could not be found. . . .

These keen knights rode out swiftly, and the King followed with five hundred more men, I would reckon. Behind them came the hunters with their feathered arrows and long bows. The nobles sounded their horns, and the deer ran out one after the other, both buck and hind. By midmorning five hundred deer were slain under the linden trees.

From morning until the middle of the afternoon Sir Gawain, Sir Kay, and Bishop Baldwin rode after a huge stag without stopping. A mist arose on the moor, and the barons kept blowing their horns loud, Sir Kay complaining that they would find no stags around there. Listen to what happened to them. By this time they wanted greatly to find shelter, and that noble knight, Sir Gawain, spoke:

"All our efforts are worthless, believe me. The deer have vanished clean out of sight. We shan't meet any more today, so please hear me. I think we should dismount and stay in this wood for the night. Let us camp under this tree."

"Let us ride on," said Sir Kay immediately. "We can find lodging before we go very far. None of you can deny that."

"I know that well," Bishop Baldwin said then. "Near at hand is a carl in the castle, the Carl of Carlisle by name. He will give us lodging, as I understand it, by St. James. But no one who was ever his guest is so hardy that he did not receive a rough welcome. Any guest will be beaten, as I heard tell, and if ever he got away with his life, it was only by the grace of God. All three of us better ride there together."

"I agree with that," Sir Kay said. "Let us do as you advise. Even if the Carl is strong, I am no more afraid of him than I am of a hare. In spite of how tough he is, we will beat him front and back and chase him from his castle. Whatever he brews, let him drink it himself. We will beat him until he bleeds. He will wish he had never run into us."

"As long as I am blessed by life," Sir Gawain said, "I will not be his guest against his will, though I could if I wished. If I speak politely, it will help us make the lord glad to have us in his own castle. Sir Kay, stop your boasting. It's been my experience you will only cause trouble. As I say, I will pray the good lord of the castle for lodging, food, and drink until tomorrow."

Quickly they rode on their way and stopped at the castle gate where a mallet to call the porter hung on a chain. Sir Kay refused to use it and would like to have jerked it off the chain, but a sour-looking porter came to the gate and asked them what they wanted. Sir Gawain replied courteously.

"We beseech the good lord of this castle for lodging."

"I will deliver the message gladly," the porter answered, "but do not blame me if you are sorry for it. You are all strong and handsome, your appearance is pleasing, but my lord does not know anything about courtesy. You will not leave from here without being insulted, believe me. I am sorry you came this way, and before you go, you will agree with me, unless God's grace intervenes."

"Porter," said Kay, "don't worry about us. You can see we cannot go any further. You are jesting with us, I suspect. But take our message to the lord. We will grab these keys away from you and let down the drawbridge ourselves."

"On my life," the porter answered, "there are not three knights alive who would dare do that. If my lord knew what you had said, some of you would lose your lives unless you can flee in a great hurry."

The porter went back to the hall and there met his lord, a rugged and strong man.

"Carl of Carlisle, God save you," the porter saluted him. "At the gate are three men, two armed like Arthur's knights, and a bishop. No more, as they told me."

"By Saint Michael," the Carl replied, "this news pleases me well, since they wished to come this way."

When the knights came before this lord, they found four frightening animals lying around the fire: a wild bull, a fierce boar, a savage lion, and a huge bear, all completely untethered around the Carl's feet. The knights were greatly startled. The animals jumped up, charged them, and would have quickly killed them but the Carl ordered them back.

"Lie down, my four whelps," he said. The lion roared and glowered like a hot coal. The bear growled, the bull snorted, and the boar whet his tusks. "Go back! Lie down!" ordered the Carl, and at these words, they obeyed him and crawled under the table, fearing him. Sir Kay took note of what happened.

The knights looked carefully at the Carl with his rugged and bold appearance. He seemed a fearful man: heavy cheeks, a broad face, a large hooked nose, and a huge mouth. He measured a span between his brows and had a gray beard as wide as a battle flag that covered his chest. The distance between his shoulders was two tailor's yards, as the story goes.

Sir Kay was stupified at the man. He was nine tailor's yards tall with long and massive legs. His thighs were thicker than any column in the hall, and his arms and fingers as powerful as ordinary legs. Anyone who could stand up under a single blow of his hand would be no weakling, I can safely swear.

As his guest Sir Gawain knelt before him, but the Carl remarked that he was not going to knight Sir Gawain—after all he was a knight already—and bade him stand up again.

"Enough of your kneeling, noble knight. You lodge with a carl tonight, I swear by St. John. You will not find any knightly courtesy here. Only carl's courtesy, so save me God. I certainly do not know any other." The Carl ordered wine in pure gold cups that shone as bright as the sun, each one holding four gallons and more. Then he had an even larger one brought in.

"Why have this little cup? When I am sitting at the high seat by the fire, it is too little for me. Bring me a bigger one. Let us really drink! Then we will enjoy ourselves until we go to supper." The butler now brought in a cup of gold that held nine gallons and took it immediately to the Carl. Anyone who could even carry it in one hand was not weak. The knights joined in the drinking and then went out to the stable to see how their horses were cared for.

The horses had been supplied grain and meal, but a little foal stood near them eating the fodder. The Bishop pulled the foal away.

"You don't eat out of my horse's trough while I am bishop here," he said. The Carl quickly came outside and asked:

"Who has done this thing?"

"It was I," said the Bishop.

"You have earned a blow on the head, I swear, so God save me, and I mean a blow to remember," the Carl replied.

"I am in holy orders," the Bishop said.

"I swear you do not know anything about courtesy." The Carl knocked the Bishop out, and he collapsed on the ground.

Sir Kay also wanted to inspect his mount, and also

finding the little horse gave him a clout across the haunches and drove him out of doors. The Carl saw this with his own eyes, and gave Kay such a buffet that he laid him out completely cold on the ground.

"You evil-learned knights," the Carl said. "I shall teach you some of my courtesy before you leave here."

When the Bishop and Sir Kay revived again, they went back into the hall, and Sir Gawain asked where they had been.

"We saw to our horses, but we are sore from doing it," they said. Then Sir Gawain said courteously:

"Sir, with your leave, then I will see to mine." The Carl already knew his thoughts.

Outside it rained and blew a terrible storm. By bell, book, and candle, anyone who had a place to stay was lucky. The foal stood outside the stable door and was dripping wet, but Gawain led him inside by the hand and covered him with his own green mantle.

"Stand up here, little horse, and eat your food. The least I can do is take care of my host's foal." The Carl was not far away and thanked him courteously many times.

By supper time the tables, set up on a platform, were immediately covered with food, and no one delayed with the meal. The Bishop sat at the head of the table happy with his place. Sir Kay sat proudly on the other side opposite the Carl's wife.

There was no lovelier woman to be found. She was beautiful and pale. Her arms were small, her waist tiny, her eyes gray, her eyebrows arched, her cheeks round. She knew perfectly how to be gracious. She was animated by nature, gloriously sparkling, and so attractively dressed that I cannot begin to describe her clothes.

"Alas, lovely lady," Sir Kay thought to himself, "that you should be wasted on such a foul man!"

"Be still," said the Carl, who could read Kay's

thoughts, "and eat your food! You are thinking more than you dare speak out, that I can tell you, all right."

I understand that no one had asked Gawain to sit down, and he remained standing in the hall.

"Friend, quickly," the Carl said to him, "do what I tell you and correctly! Take a spear in your hand and stand at the buttery door, then hit me in the face with it. Do as I command, now! If you pin me against the wall, you won't hurt me at all, while I am a giant here on earth." Sir Gawain was glad to comply. At the buttery door he picked up the spear, took it in his hand, and charged with all his strength. The Carl ducked his head, and the spear crashed into the stone wall with such force that it shattered, sparks jumping out of the flint head. Not hesitating, the Carl said to him:

"Noble knight, you have done well," and he took him by the hand. A chair was fetched for Sir Gawain, that worthy knight of Britain, and he sat at the table in front of the Carl's wife. His love was so drawn to her that he could neither eat nor drink.

"Gawain, take comfort," the Carl said. "She is lovely, I know that, and I speak honestly. She, who you want for your own, is mine. Give up your fancy and drink some wine, for you will never get her." Sir Gawain was ashamed of what he had been thinking.

The Carl's daughter, beautiful and appealing, was then escorted into the hall. Her hair was like gold. Her dress was magnificently ornamented, decorated with rich jewels and pearls and cost more than a thousand pounds. Her beauty and her dress both shone in the hall like beams of the sun.

"Where is the harp that you should have carried with you?" the Carl asked this lovely girl. "Why did you forget it?" It was brought into the hall immediately, and a splendid chair was set before her father. The harp was of fine maple wood, and I believe the pins were of gold. With no further delay she played the harp and sang of love and of Arthur's knights and how they met at the Round Table.

When all had supped and been entertained, the Bishop was led into his chamber and with him Sir Kay. They showed Sir Gawain to the Carl's own chamber, which was bright and resplendent, and asked him to go to bed under a cloth of brilliant gold spread on the bed when it was to be used for pleasure. A squire came in secretly who helped Sir Gawain disarm and undress. Then the Carl asked his own wife to go into the chamber.

"Sir Gawain," he said, "take my wife in your two arms and kiss her in my presence."

"Sir, your will shall be carried out," Sir Gawain answered him quickly, "even if you strike me, knock me down, or kill me." Gawain went right to the bed, for the softness of the lady's body made him want to do what the Carl ordered and the Carl knew it. But when Gawain would have done the secret deed, the Carl said:

"Whoa there! That game I forbid! But, Gawain, since you have done what I asked, I must show you kindness in something at least. You shall have a girl as good looking who will be yours until tomorrow." He went to his daughter's chamber and ordered her to go to the knight and deny nothing he asked for. The girl did not dare go against her father's bidding but immediately went to Gawain and lay down beside him submissively.

"Now, Gawain," said the Carl, "I give my blessing on you two. I think you will find joy together."

Sir Gawain was happy because of this beautiful girl, I can tell you in truth.

"Mary mercy!" the girl thought, "I never knew a knight like this before."

In the morning Sir Kay arose and wished to take his horse and return home.

"No, Sir Kay," the Bishop said, "we will not leave

until we have seen Sir Gawain." The Carl arose and found the meal he ordered fully prepared. Then the bell for mass rang. Sir Gawain kissed his beautiful girl, arose, and went to mass.

"Mary mercy!" the girl said, "where shall I ever see this knight again?" After the mass Sir Gawain took his leave and thanked the Carl for his hospitality.

"First," said the Carl, "you shall all dine and all go homeward together with my blessing. It has been twenty years since I made a vow to God for which I was sad. I vowed that any man, whether lord or commoner, who ever lodged in my castle would be slain unless he did as he was ordered. Gawain, I found no one except you who did as I ordered. Now may God in Heaven give you happiness, and I am glad, for you have changed my grief to joy, through the help of Mary, Queen of Heaven."

The Carl led Sir Gawain to a lonely hut where they found ten cartloads of men's bones and many bloody tabards each with a different coat of arms. It was a hideous sight.

"Gawain, I slew all these men, I and my four animals, and I am telling you the truth. But now I shall forsake my evil ways. No one will be slain here ever again. As far as I am able, everyone who comes this way will be welcomed, because of the respect I have for you. I will erect a chantry here for the souls of all those who have died, and ten priests will sing masses for their souls until judgment day."

Dinner was prepared by that time, the table set up and covered with food. Sir Gawain and his radiant lady were served together, and there was great merrymaking between them, which made the Carl happy. He told the Bishop and Sir Kay that they, too, should be happy. In return for the Bishop's blessing the Carl gave him a cross, a miter, a ring, and a cloth of gold. He gave Sir

Kay, the irascible knight, a blood-red steed, a faster one that Sir Kay had ever seen.

Then he gave his daughter to Gawain and with her a white palfrey and a packhorse loaded with gold. The girl was so glorious and dazzling I could not even describe her. Really, she was more exquisite than any girl in the world.

"Now ride out, Gawain," the Carl ordered, "with my blessing, and give my greeting to Arthur, your king. And ask Arthur, for the love of Him who was born in Bethlehem, that he dine with me tomorrow." Gawain promised he would. Gawain and the beautiful girl with all the knights rode away singing, and they reported to King Arthur where they had been and what extraordinary adventure had occurred to them.

"Now God be thanked, cousin Gawain," said Arthur, "that you escaped unslain. I say that with all my heart."

"I escaped too, Sir King," Sir Kay added, "and I have never been so glad about anything in my life. And the Carl prayed that for the love of Him born in Bethlehem, you should dine with him tomorrow."

Arthur promised he would, and at dawn they rode out. A royal meeting was made with many of the noble knights. At the gate of the Carl's castle they were greeted with the sound of silver trumpets, harps, fiddles, psalteries, lutes, gitterns, and the minstrelsy accompanied them into the castle. The Carl knelt down and welcomed the King befittingly. When the King was accompanied into the hall, he found nothing imaginable lacking. The walls gleamed like glass, a glittering pattern of gold, azure, and gray. The niches of the hall were decorated with gold that no one could praise enough. After a flourish of trumpets, the King said grace and ordered the banquet to begin. Without delay swans, pheasants, cranes, partridges, plovers, and curlews were set before them. To the King the Carl said:

"You will never see any greater courtesy than this," and he ordered golden bowls brought in so great that no single knight who was there was able to lift any with his one hand.

"By Saint Michael," the King swore, "this dinner pleases me as much as any I have ever seen." In the morning he dubbed the Carl as knight and gave him the country of Carlisle as his own land.

"And at this moment I make you a knight of the Round Table; Carlisle shall be your name." And as the sun rose that morning, Sir Gawain married the beautiful girl. The Carl was overjoyed and thanked the King many times. The feasting lasted a fortnight with games, pleasure, and entertainment. The minstrels were given gifts, so they played their best, and the knights only went home when it was all finally complete.

In the pleasant town of Carlisle the Carl built a rich abbey to sing and say mass for the worship of God and of our Lady, built so strong and well that it became cathedral town. In it Franciscans chant and say mass until the last judgment for the men that the Carl has slain. And may Christ in Heaven above bring us all to bliss.

The Green Knight

Introduction

The most famous story of Sir Gawain involves his adventures with the Green Knight. Two versions of this romance have survived. The earlier version, one preserved in a fourteenth-century manuscript in the British Museum, Cotton Nero A x, has been edited several times, is often reprinted and modernized. It is an aristocratic version meant to be read at a court to an audience of knights and ladies.

This modernization is based on a manuscript 200 years later in the Bishop Percy Folio. Not as widely known as *Sir Gawain and the Green Knight,* this version has never before been translated. It is a popular version meant for everyday people—a group at a pilgrims' inn, at a tavern, or at a village square on market day. The story moves faster than in the aristocratic version, the action is more succinct, and the basic conflict is more clearly defined. Sir Gawain has to pit his knightly skill against the witchcraft of Agostes, the Green Knight's mother-in-law. This situation is defined from the beginning of the story, and so the audience understands and anticipates the conflict. The listener is told that Gawain's ability as a fighter alone will not help him save his life. Still, no one questions that he will keep his word and meet the Green Knight for the second of the two blows. When Kay volunteers for the challenge, he is denied it, for the members of Arthur's court all know that Kay might not be true to his word while Gawain would be. The contrast between Kay and Gawain illustrates the knightly virtue of truth.

The audience is interested in the tale not because of suspense about how it will end. No one expects Sir Gawain to be killed. The interest lies in the dilemma: how can Sir Gawain escape with his life and still accept the sword blow from the Green Knight? The magic of the lace offers a solution to that and to overcoming the witchcraft of Agostes.

At the beginning of the story we learn the origin of the Round Table. In the Middle Ages rank, or degree, was by no means clear cut. Knighthood was not an inherited rank, and a knight could be connected differently to various persons outside of knighthood who affected his degree in different ways. Fights at table over rank occurred in several Irish and Welsh stories. In a chronicle of the early thirteenth century, the *Brut* by Layamon, a priest of King's Areley on the Severn River, Layamon gives a vivid picture of the argument at the Round Table. The quarrel among the knights broke out at Christmas. It started with their throwing loaves of bread and progressed to silver wine bowls and eventually to fists. Creating a Round Table settled the argu-

ment of rank, for all the knights could now sit in a circle
with no one being at the head of the table.

The story of the Round Table in this tale provided
the audience with a sense of history, and the specific
place-names provided a sense of geography. King Arthur, like all other kings in the Middle Ages, moved
from castle to castle as provisions at each were deplet-
ed. In this tale he moves from a castle in Cheshire, not
identifiable today, to Carlisle. Sir Bredbeddle and Sir
Gawain stayed at Hutton Manor in Somersetshire. This
manor exists, its great hall going back to the fifteenth
century.

The reference at the end of the tale to the Knights
of the Bath apparently also had some validity. The great
orders of the Garter and of the Bath, as well as similar
orders in France and Germany, were attempts to revive
and to strengthen the ideals of knighthood which, even
in the fourteenth century, were being eroded, as noted
in the general introduction.

The Bishop Percy Folio Manuscript, in which the
"Green Knight," as well as other versions of the "Carl
of Carlisle" and the "Wedding of Dame Ragnell," was
discovered, having just barely survived from the seven-
teenth century. Thomas Percy, not then the Bishop of
Dromore in Ireland, rescued the manuscript from a
housemaid who was using it to start the morning fires.
He edited the manuscript and published it in 1765. It
is from a later, more careful editing that these first two
stanzas are reprinted.

> List! wen Arthur he was King,
> he had all att his leadinge
> the broad Ile of Brittaine;
> England & Scottland one was,
> & wales stood in the same case,
> the truth itt is not to layne.

he drive allyance out of this Ile,
soe Arthur liued in peace a while,
as men of Mickle maine,
knights strong of their degree
[strove] which of them hyest shold bee;
therof Arthur was not faine;

The Tale

I

Listen! When Arthur was king and had the broad Isle of Britain under his rule, England and Scotland were one and Wales was in the same kingdom. He had driven all the foreigners out of the land, so Arthur a while lived in peace. His knights, all men of great strength, quarreled with one another about their rank, who should be seated highest at table. Arthur was not

39

happy about this, so he made a round table. It was for their own good that none of them should sit above the other, but around it they sat as equals. The King himself sat on a royal throne with Dame Guenevere, a woman beautiful in face and figure.

At one Christmas time it happened that many knights came to the royal castle bringing their helmets and swords with them, and they were received into the order of knighthood at that time. There was no castle or manor that could accommodate them all, their number was so great, and they pitched tents where they could both eat and sleep. Messengers went back and forth between the tents carrying the best of food, wines, and wild fowl, and the knights did not spare anything that gold was able to buy.

I am not going to talk about King Arthur any more right now but I will tell you about an adventurous knight who lived in the west country. Sir Bredbeddle was his true name. He was a man of great power, a handsome lord, and had a wife whom he loved dearly, a lady spirited and attractive. Because Sir Gawain was so great in tourneys, secretly she loved him, but she had never seen him.

Agostes, her mother, was a witch. If any person, a knight or an ordinary man, had been wounded lightly or grievously, or even slain in battle, she could cure him. She told her son-in-law that he should take a journey but with his appearance completely changed.

"You shall go to Arthur's hall," she told him, "for great adventures shall befall you there that no one ever saw before." All these plans were for her daughter's sake. Because her daughter loved Sir Gawain, Agostes wanted to bring him to her castle to meet her.

"On my life," the knight answered, "I will go to Arthur's court and test Gawain in three ways to see if it's true what people say about him, by Mary most powerful."

As soon as it was dawn, the knight dressed himself in his best and mounted one of his finer steeds. He took his helmet, his mail, and his long broadsword to use if it was necessary. He made an extraordinary sight, for his horse, weapons, and armor were all green, and when he was completely dressed, I truly swear, even his complexion took on the same color.

At that time Arthur the King rode to Carlisle after he had left Flatting Castle in the forest of Delamere, Cheshire. And Sir Bredbeddle rode to Carlisle, arriving on Christmas day. At the gate the porter thought he was an incredible sight and asked him:

"Sir, where do you wish to go?"

"I am a knight on an adventure," the knight replied, "and wish to see your king and the other lords that are here." The porter did not answer a word but left him standing at the gate. He knelt before the King and said:

"In all my born days, I have never seen such a person. For at your gate yonder is a venturous knight, but everything about him is green."

"Bring him into the hall," the King replied, "and let us see what all this is about." When the Green Knight came before the King, he stood up in his stirrups and spoke out in a loud voice:

"King Arthur, God save you and keep you in prosperity and honor. Because you wish me nothing but what is right, I have come here venturously and have traveled into your country to test the courage of your lords in your palace."

"As I am a true knight and king," the King replied willingly, "you shall have what you ask. I will not deny it, whether you wish to fight on foot or to tilt on horseback for the love of a lady. If you do not have good armor, I will give you part of mine."

"Great thanks to you, my lord," he answered. "I make my challenge here among all the lords, young and old, magnificently dressed, which of them then will take this in hand, which of them is both courageous and strong, and which skilled when the need comes. I shall lay down my head, and he can strike it a single blow, if he's able. But this day twelfth month he will let me give him another blow at his own head. Let me see who will answer this, some knight who is valiant. For this day twelfth month, to tell the truth, let him come to me to keep his promise without hesitation. I shall tell him the shortest way to the Green Chapel where I shall be."

The King sat still, and during all this time his lords said little. Then Sir Kay stood up, that crabbed knight, and spoke loudly and shrilly:

"I shall strike his neck in two, loose his head from his body." The others told him to be still.

"Kay, don't start swaggering about this," they said. "You don't know what you are getting into. It is nothing good, but a great ill." Still each of the lords wished the challenge were answered.

Then Sir Gawain knelt before Arthur and said:

"It would be a great discourtesy unless you, my liege, awarded this deed to me. Remember, I am your sister's son."

"I grant your boon," the King said, "but joy is better at a feast. Cheer your guest, give him wine, and after the dinner give him your blow and do it well."

For the banquet the Green Knight was seated at the Round Table and served fittingly. He did not talk about his business and took only the time necessary for the meal. When the dinner was over, the King said to Sir Gawain:

"If you wish now to do your deed, I pray Jesus for your success. This knight looks enduring." The Green

Knight laid his head down, and Sir Gawain swung the axe and struck the neck bone in two. Blood burst out of every vein, and the head fell off the body.

But the Green Knight picked up his head and holding it, sprang into his saddle.

"Gawain," the head spoke loudly and sharply, "think on your agreement. For this day a year be sure you come to the Green Chapel." Everyone, the King, knights, and lords, had seen that awesome sight, the head speaking so blithely as the knight held it by the hair and then rode out the hall door. Only when he was outside the door did the Green Knight set his head on his body again. Then he turned and said:

"Arthur, hear my promise. Whenever your knight visits me, I'll guarantee him a better blow than that, for sure." The Green Knight rode away. All this was accomplished by the enchantment of the old witch.

Arthur the King grew melancholy and mourned greatly that Sir Gawain was brought into conflict with such evil. The Queen wept for him, and Sir Lancelot du Lake and the others also grieved, because Sir Gawain had been brought into this terrible peril. His great strength, which before had won his tourneys, would not help him in this situation. Sir Gawain comforted the King and Queen and all the nobles assembled there. He ordered them to be still.

"I was never afraid of what I was doing," he said, "I swear by St. Michael. For when the day comes, I will arm myself and keep my promise. But, sir," he added, "I do not know where this Green Chapel is, and I wish to seek it out." The royal court all understood this and thought it for the best. The knights left the castle for the fields around, took their spears and shields, and made themselves ready. Some went jousting, some dancing, some reveling and singing. And they all swore together that if Sir Gawain were overcome, they would burn all the west country.

Now we must leave the King in his palace. The Green Knight came home into his castle, and his people asked him what great deeds he had accomplished, but he would tell them nothing. He knew well that his wife with so beautiful a face and figure loved Sir Gawain.

Listen, lordlings, if you will stay seated, you will hear the second part and what further adventures befell Sir Gawain.

II

The day arrived that Gawain must depart, and at the castle the knights and ladies grew pale. The King himself sighed mournfully, and the Queen almost swooned, all because of this journey that Gawain had to undertake.

In his bright armor he was one of the handsomest knights that was ever in Britain. They brought him a dapple-gray steed, a good one, I can tell you. The bridle was set with precious stones decorated with gold, pearls, and stones of great worth. They were marvelous trappings. I can say truly that his stirrups were of Indian silk. When he rode over the land, his gear dazzled golden in the sun.

As he rode along to seek the Green Chapel, he saw many astonishing sights. All the birds flew away from the shore along the sea coast. He saw wolves and other wild beasts, and he hunted as he went. One evening he was riding on a path and saw a magnificent castle. Turning toward it, he arrived at sunset and met a noble knight, the lord of the place.

"For Arthur's sake," Sir Gawain asked him humbly, "I beg you for repose. I am a knight who has labored far, and I pray you to lodge me for the night." The knight did not deny him but took him by the arm into the hall and ordered a groom to care for his horse. The host and Sir Gawain went together into one of the smaller chambers where everything was prepared. A fire was burning brightly, candles in their candelabra.

Joyously they went to supper, and the lord sent for his lady to join them. Eagerly she arrived followed by her ladies-in-waiting, all in rich gowns of purple. As she sat at the banquet, always the attractive lady, Sir Gawain could not take his eyes from her, but when supper was over, she took her ladies and retired to her chamber.

Then the lord cheered Sir Gawain with wine and said:

"Welcome, by St. Martin. I pray you, and do not take it ill, why have you ridden so far this way, if you will tell me? I am a knight as well as you, and if you tell me, I will keep personal whatever you say. But if anything worries you, perhaps I may be able to help you." If Gawain had known the truth of the matter, in spite of the host's friendly words, he would not have told him, for the host was the Green Knight, and Gawain was lodged at his own castle.

"As to the Green Chapel," Sir Bredbeddle told Sir Gawain, "I can tell you how to get there. It is only three furlongs off. The master of it is an adventurous knight who practices witchcraft day and night and can produce many a great spell. He is clever and can be courteous if he wishes. You shall stay here a while, take your rest while I hunt in the greenwood forest nearby." And they made a pact between them that whatever God sent either one, whether it was worth gold and silver or nothing at all, they would exchange it.

While the Green Knight went hunting, Sir Gawain stayed in the castle sleeping in his bed. Then the old witch arose early and went to her daughter.

"Don't be afraid," she said, "but the man you have wanted for many a day is in the castle. Now you can have him. Sir Gawain, the courteous knight, is lodging here all night." She brought her daughter to his bed and said, "Gentle knight, awake for the sake of this beautiful lady, who has loved you dearly. Take her in your arms, and no harm will come to you."

The lady kissed him three times and said to him:

"Unless I have your love, I will be sorry my whole life long."

Sir Gawain blushed and replied:

"Your husband is a noble knight, as Christ is my witness. I would be ashamed if I brought any grief to this man who has been kind to me. I have a pledge to keep, and I can have no rest or quiet until it is accomplished."

"Tell me something of your journey," the lady then asked him. "Perhaps I can help you. If it has something to do with war, no man will be able to harm you, if you follow my advice. Here I have a silken lace, as white as milk and valuable. I swear that no man shall harm you when you have it with you." Gawain answered graciously, thanked the lady, took the lace, and promised to see her again.

In the forest and meadows Sir Bredbeddle slew many hinds, wild boars, swine, and foxes in the ravine. That evening Sir Gawain greeted him.

"Welcome to your home, in the name of Christ, who harrowed Hell." The Green Knight laid his venison down at Gawain's feet.

"Now tell me right away what novelties have you won?" he said. "Here is venison aplenty."

"Such as God has given me, you shall have your share," Sir Gawain answered and swore by St. Leonard. He took the knight in his arms and kissed him three times. "This is what God sent me, by Mary the great." But secretly he kept the lace, and that was the only dishonor that was ever proved against Sir Gawain.

That night they retired and slept through until the

next day. Then Sir Gawain graciously took his leave of
the lady, thanking her for the lace that he took with
him. Though he did not know the way, he rode toward
the Green Chapel, and as he rode, he wondered if he
should do as the lady told him. At the same time Sir
Bredbeddle rode another way now, changed into his
green hue as he was before.

Sir Gawain rode over the plain, and as he crossed
a mountain, he heard a horn blow loud. He looked for
the Green Chapel and saw it standing under a hill covered with yews. He looked for the Green Knight and
saw him whetting his broadsword so the hills echoed
with the noise.

The Green Knight spoke directly:

"You are welcome here, Sir Gawain, and it be-
hooves you to lower your head." Then the Green
Knight swung his sword but only nicked the skin a little,
hardly touching the flesh.

"You flinched," the Green Knight said. "Why did
you?"

Then Gawain took heart. He stood up on his feet
and quickly drew his sword.

"Traitor!" he said, "if you object by a word, your
life is in my hand. I had only one strike at you, and you
one at me. You know this is no lie."

"I think I might have killed Sir Gawain," the knight
answered, "the noblest knight in all this land. People
told me of his renown. You might have worn the crown
for courtesy above everyone else, noble, yeoman, or
commoner. But now I put three charges to you, more's
the pity. Sir Gawain, you were not loyal, honorable, or
true when you concealed the lace that my wife gave
you. We had both pledged, you know well, and you
received half of my hunting. But even if you had never
taken the lace, I wouldn't have slain you. Truly, I swear
by God. I knew well my wife loved you. But you would

not have cuckolded me. You told her no. Now I ask you, take me to Arthur's court with you, and I will be content."

The two knights agreed to this and went on to the Castle of Hutton and stayed there the night. Early the next day they continued on their way to Arthur's court with light and happy hearts. There all the court was glad to see Gawain alive, and for this they thanked God above.

This is the reason why each Knight of the Bath wears the lace until he has won his spurs or until a lady of high rank shall take it from his neck for all the brave deeds that he has done. It was confirmed by Arthur the King through the wish of Sir Gawain. The King granted him his request.

So ends the tale of the Green Knight. May God, who is so mighty, bring to Heaven the souls of all those who have heard this little tale that happened in the west country in the days of Arthur our King.

The Adventures
at Tarn Wadling

Introduction

These two adventures, one at Tarn Wadling, one near Carlisle, are typical of medieval stories, but they have less in common with modern fiction than do "Sir Gawain and the Carl of Carlisle" and "The Green Knight." The two adventures, for example, are not psychologically related as the twentieth-century reader would demand they be. One incident does not seem to effect the other, and no reference is made from one to the other until after Sir Galeron becomes a knight of the Round Table. Then Queen Guenevere, as she said she would, commands masses be said for her mother, the ghost who appears in the first adventure.

For the fifteenth century, however, it was enough that the same people are involved in both adventures and that both adventures take place in the same general location, though this last fact is not as important in supporting the concepts the Middle Ages had of unity. That the two adventures present two pictures of life, life after death and life before, gave a sense of completeness to the audience of the fifteenth century. Or, as Professor David Klausner has suggested, the two adventures are really examples of punishment for two of the sins mentioned in the ghost's sermon: the sin of *luxuria*, licentiousness, as seen in the punishment of Guenevere's mother, and of *avaritia*, avarice, as seen in the defeat of Sir Galeron on earth.

Our great emphasis on unity is a modern criterion. The Middle Ages in their narratives asked for entertainment combined with teaching. The audience did not object to a story being "interspersed" with sermons, proverbs, anecdotes, or fables, as we can observe all through the *Canterbury Tales*. The sermon the ghost delivered emphasizes common moral teachings, the imminence of death, and the importance of generosity, one of the cardinal knightly and theological virtues.

Guenevere's mother is a typical medieval ghost. A modern ghost, like those found in the writings of Edgar Allan Poe, H. R. Lovecraft, Shirley Jackson, or M. R. James, is psychological and exists primarily to frighten the reader. In the Middle Ages ghosts are inhabitants of a theological universe and appear on earth to teach eternal truths.

This medieval ghost has a literary tradition. We find such ghosts in *De casibus virorum illustrium (The Fates of Illustrious Men)*, Boccaccio's most famous work before the sixteenth century discovered the *Decameron*. In *The Fates*, illustrious men from Adam through King Arthur appear who tell why they suffered their punishments. The ghostly tradition also emerges in

Elizabethan drama in Macbeth's three witches and in the ghost of Hamlet's father.

Ghosts have a limited knowledge of the future, as Dante explained in the *Inferno,* and in this tradition Guenevere's mother predicts the death of Gawain, the death of Arthur, and the dissolution of the Round Table. The story she told was well known to the audience and could have been found in Geoffrey of Monmouth's *Histories,* mentioned in the general introduction. Probably the teller of "The Adventures at Tarn Wadling" took the prophecies from the great English epic of the Middle Ages, the alliterative *Morte Arthure* (not to be confused with Sir Thomas Malory's *Le Morte d'Arthur* of the fifteenth century).

The ghost alludes to the story of Arthur's campaign against the Romans, Modred's treason in England while Arthur is fighting on the continent, and the final battle between the forces of Modred and those of the Round Table, when in one day, all the knights of the Round Table are killed. The cause of the downfall, the ghost says, was Arthur's greed in conquering the world. The love of Guenevere and Lancelot as a cause for the downfall of the Round Table is a much later interpretation popularized in Tennyson's *Idylls of the King* during the nineteenth century. In "The Adventures at Tarn Wadling" Sir Gawain is the Queen's special knight, a position he occupied in early romances.

A tarn was an appropriate setting for the appearance of the ghost. The word itself was borrowed into English from Old Norse and was used to describe a mountain lake without visible feeders or outlets, the waters of which are dark and the shores of which are marshy.

Guenevere's mother does not seem to have a fictional history that has survived, so we do not know what vow it was she broke. Guenevere, like Gawain and Kay, is mentioned in the *Mabinogion,* where her name is Gwenhwyfar. The manuscripts of the "The Adventures" spell her name variously Gaynor, Gaynoure, or Waynour, among others, but for this modernization I use the more familiar spelling that came into English from the French.

The second of the adventures, the joust between Sir Galeron and Sir Gawain, introduces us to the mail and plate armor of the midfourteenth century, the time of the battles of Crécy and Poitiers. As mentioned in the general introduction, at the time these manuscripts were being written the mail and plate combination had been supplanted by plate alone. Of course, the jewels which came off in the fight were an idealized exaggeration. The best plate was smooth so weapons would slide off of it, and jewels would catch the blow of a sword or lance.

If the armor the knights fought in was archaic, the furnishings of Sir Galeron's enormous pavilion would be recognized as up-to-date. The storyteller mentioned the stove had a chimney, for example, and chimneys, even in castles, were not general before the fourteenth century. The wine at Arthur's banquet was served not only in cups but also in glasses, a rare elegance before the time of Henry VIII.

Sir Galeron is not a prominent figure in any tale. We saw he was mentioned as one of the knights accompanying King Arthur for the hunt that began "Sir Gawain and the Carl of Carlisle." He first appears in French romances as Galeran, and a Galerians of the White Tower is mentioned as an uncle of Perceval. In Sir Thomas Malory, Sir Galleron of Galloway is defeated by Sir Palomydes, but when he lends his armor to Sir Tristram, then Tristram defeats Palomydes. The storyteller would not feel obliged to maintain any consistency with earlier works, even if he knew them, when he used a name as little known as this one.

"The Adventures of Tarn Wadling" is preserved in four manuscripts of the fifteenth century. The dialect varies from manuscript to manuscript, of course, but all of them have characteristics of the North of England and to a lesser extent some of those of the West Midlands. This translation is based primarily on the Thornton manuscript in the library of Lincoln Cathedral. The verse form, as can be seen in the stanza here, is rhymed alliteratively. The verse has basically four stresses of which three are alliterated. This was a prominent form of English verse from *Beowulf* to the sixteenth century.

> In Kyng Arthure tym ane awntir by-tyde,
> By the Terne Wahethelyn, als the buke tellis,
> Als he to Carelele was comen, that conqueroure
>   kyde,
> With dukes, and wt ducheperes, þat wt þat dere
>   duellys,
> For to hunte at the herdys þat lange hase bene
>   hyde;
> And one a daye þay þam dighte to þe depe dellis,
> To felle of þe femmales in þe foreste wele fry-
>   thede,
> Faire in the fernysone tyme, by frythis and fellis.
> Thus to þe wode are thay wente, the wlonkeste
>   in wedys,
> Bothe the kynge and the qwene,
> And all be doghety by-dene,
> Syr Gawane, gayeste one grene,
> Dame Gayenoure he ledis.

The Tale

I

In the days of King Arthur, as the book tells us, an adventure occurred by the dark waters of Tarn Wadling. Arthur, renowned conqueror, with his duke and lords who dwelled there, had arrived at Carlisle to hunt a herd of deer unsighted for a long time. They rode into a deep valley one day and drove the hinds, well concealed among the trees, into the open moors beside the streams, the kind of hunting allowed during this season.

All of the hunters were superbly dressed, both the King, the Queen, and their companions. Best of all, Sir Gawain in green, led Queen Guenevere, their apparel glittering, flashing with ribbons and faced with silk. Those who read about it also learn their clothing dazzled with rubies. Dame Guenevere's blue hood, covering her head, was lined with fur and laced with the most precious gems. Her short coat, proof against rain, in truth, was embroidered with sapphires. She rode on a white mule, and her saddle, covered with silk, was as elegant as her dress. Everyone in the party was attired in the same wondrous manner.

And so, glistening in jewels, she and Sir Gawain on a white charger from Burgundy, rode along the paths until they came to a tarn. They continued along its shores and in a vale they dismounted under a laurel tree. At the same time King Arthur and his earls were riding hard. Arthur assigned hunting stations, and each of the lords with a bow and arrows and blood hounds settled down in these stations beneath the trees at the foot of a bank. Here these lords waited for any hinds that were barren during this season while they listened for the sound of the hunting horns and quieted the hounds. Then they loosed the hounds which made their kill.

With fresh hounds they followed after the herd and pursued their quest through the valleys and along fast-moving streams they had not seen before. The hunters hallooed through the woods and glens, their greyhounds giving the deer no rest. They charged wild boars, which was the boars' undoing. Finally, the King, eagerly following the chase with his sergeant-at-arms, blew on his horn to assemble the hounds, and the nobles joined their sovereign in the forest, happy to be together.

All the knights assembled except Gawain who remained with Guenevere in the green copse. They rested in a grove of thick boxberries and shrubs beneath the laurel. Close by this grove something awesome took place that I want to tell you about. The day became dark as midnight. The King, astounded, leapt from his horse, and the other knights dismounted in fright and fled from the woods to the rocks to escape a violent rain, sleet, and snow that cracked at them.

Out of the tarn—and I hold nothing back—a creature arose, something like Lucifer, the most frightening devil of Hell, and it glided toward Sir Gawain and Guenevere howling, yammering, and shrieking while at the same time it was weeping.

"I curse the body that bore me," it said. "Woe! My suffering consumes me. I fear and mourn." The ghost made so frightening a clamor even the huge greyhounds cowered and ran into the brush to cover their heads. In the trees birds shrieked their warning. Dame Guenevere was frightened and asked Sir Gawain what they ought to do.

"This only comes from an eclipse of the sun I heard a scholar talk once about," he answered trying to comfort her.

"Sir Cador, Sir Kay, and the other knights are villainous, I swear by the cross and the creed," Guenevere said. "They have left me on my death-day here with the most appalling ghost I ever heard."

"Do not worry about the ghost," said Sir Gawain. "I shall speak with it and learn what it wants. Perhaps I can quiet the woes of that gaunt corpse."

The body of the thing was bare. Its only clothing was smoke, its dark bones visible but smeared hideously with clay. It wailed and groaned like a banshee, screeching madly. It hesitated in its movement toward them, then stood fixed like a rock, pained, confused, and staring insanely. Sir Gawain went up to it, for he was never timid, as those who read about him say. A toad gnawed at the side of the specter's throat. Its eyes were hollow pits, glowing like coals. Snakes circled around close by, but to describe this thing any further would tear out my tongue.

The chivalrous knight did not change his expression but drew out his sword challenging the spirit with the crosslike hilt. The ghost's jawbone and all its face shook. Sir Gawain protected himself by calling on Christ:

"In the name of Thou who wast crucified to save us from sin, you, spirit, tell me the truth. Where are you going? Why are you walking along the paths of these woods?"

"Once I was the fairest of women," it replied, "was christened and anointed. I was related to kings renowned and powerful. God has sent me this grace to purge my sins, and now I have come to speak to your queen. For once I was a queen myself, and my face was more sparkling than any jewel, and I was more beautiful than even Brangwayne, the beauteous maid to Iseult of the White Hands. I enjoyed all the pleasures and possessions of the world, more power than Guenevere, more treasure and gold, more lands, lakes, fields, parks, more towns, castles, mountains, and valleys. But now I am separated from my family, exiled to eternal cold. Now I am trapped in pain. My bed is the damp clay. Lo, courteous knight, see what sorrowful death has done to me. But give me the sight of Guenevere, so happy." Sir Gawain went to Guenevere and brought that vivacious girl to the grisly spirit.

"Welcome, Guenevere," the spirit said, "so honored among the living. Look what death has done to your mother. Once my skin had more color than a rose blooming in the rain. My face was soft as a lily, and I laughed easily. Now I am brought down with Lucifer into this tarn and even look like him. Take me for his witness. For all your freshness, I am your mirror of the future and the mirror for every king and emperor as well. Death will do this to you, have no doubt. You should heed my appearance while you are here on earth, while you are elegantly dressed and riding around with your friends.

"But as powerful as you are, and everywhere surrounded by young men and women, have sympathy on the poor. When your body is embalmed and lying on its bier, then your friends will desert you in a great hurry. When you are brought low, then nothing will help you but holy prayers, and it will be the prayers of the poor that will bring you peace, the prayers of those unfortunates to whom you give at your gate while you sit on your throne, laughing, banqueting on all kinds of delicacies.

"While you eat those dainties at the high table, I endure terrible agonies down here. Foul, miserable, and naked, every night a gang of fiends chases after me. They drag me around and hack at me with knives. In molten brass and brimstone, I flame as if I were being cast like a bell. No person in the world is more miserable than I am. It would rip out my tongue to describe my torments—but now I want to talk about my punishment before I go. Think heartily on this and try to mend your errors. You are truly warned; beware of my woes."

"I sorrow for your sorrow," said Guenevere. "But I would know one thing more, if it is your will. If prayers and masses can help you, or any of my earthly luxuries, I would be much happier. Or if the prayers of bishops might assist you to Paradise, or those of monks. If you are my mother, it is astonishing to me that your body, once so full of life, is now charred and gaunt."

"My body bore you all right," the spirit answered.

"I have no reason to lie. But once I broke a solemn vow, and no one knew it but you and I. By this sign you know that I am telling the truth."

"But tell me truthfully," Guenevere continued, "what can help your sorrows? I will go and find saints for you against those horrible demons that bite on you and have turned you to charcoal. All this chills my blood, your skin is so burned."

"This is what happens when you take lovers, indulge your lusts and delights," said the ghost. "These made me a spirit so I belong low in this tarn. All the wealth in the world eventually goes away. This world is changeable. Worms in death now work their revenge, Guenevere. Were a trental of masses, thirty times thirty, said between morning and noon, then my soul would be saved, and I would be brought to Heavenly bliss."

"May He bring you to bliss," replied Guenevere, "who bought you dearly crucified on the cross and crowned with thorns. You were once christened, anointed, rightfully baptised. Mary the mighty, still mildest in demeanor, of whom the joyous child was born in Bethlehem, give me the grace that I may help your soul with morning prayers and masses."

"It would fill a great need," the spirit replied, "to help us with masses. But, too, in the name of Him who died on the cross, always give to those who need food while you are here on earth."

"Now I offer my hand sincerely to honor your requests, to remember you with a million masses. But one more word," said Dame Guenevere, "I would like to know. What grieves Christ more than any other thing?"

"Pride with all its accessories, as the prophets have told everyone with their preaching. Pride bears a bitter fruit for those who break God's laws. Therefore be strong to resist, for whoever resists God's bidding is deprived of all bliss. Ere a person leaves the world, he must care for his soul, Guenevere, truly."

"Tell me, a word if you know," Guenevere asked, "what deeds might best bring me to eternal joy?"

"Meekness and mercy," the ghost said, "these are the most important. Have pity on the poor, then you will please our King. And after that, perform other acts of mercy. These are the gifts of the Holy Ghost that will inspire all souls unsparingly to come to everlasting bliss. But ask me no more about these spiritual things. As you are queen in your court, hold these words in your heart. You shall live but a little while, then you will travel here."

"But what will happen to us," Gawain now asked, "who wish to fight, who often massacre people in other lands, who wrongfully conquer rich kingdoms, who win respect and honor in war through the power of our weapons?"

"Your king is too greedy," the spirit told him, "I warn you, Sir Knight. But no one has the strength to prevent him while his power remains. But at the very time he enjoys the height of his majesty and is most powerful, he shall fall low on the shore of the sea. In this way your chivalrous King shall take his chance, choose false Fortune in his wars, the wonderful goddess who guides her wheel up or down. In your wars you conquered France, King Frollo and King Feraunt left dead on the field. Brittany and Burgundy surrendered to you, and the twelve peers of France were undone, hardly a lord in France left alive.

"Then you shall overrun the powerful Romans and the Round Table will take over their wealth. But then everything will be lost, caused by a great wrath. Go, Sir Gawain, go back to Tuscany. You shall lose Britain, because of one strong knight. A knight will be truly crowned at Carlisle, but he will bring great sorrow and strife to Britain. While you are in Tuscany, you will learn of this treason. You will return home again because of the news. And there the Round Table will lose its great renown. Beside Ramsey and in Dorsetshire the most valiant of all knights shall die.

"Get you on your way, Sir Gawain, most valiant in Britain. You shall be killed in a steep valley. Such terrible things are going to happen. I am not speaking in fables. Arthur, the noble, honorable, and skilled, will be killed on the coast of Cornwall, I know. He shall be wounded badly by a powerful knight. All the noble companions of the Round Table shall die in one day, all at the same time. They will be tricked by one who owes you allegiance, one bearing a shield of black sable, on it a saltire, engrailed in silver. This is the arms he bears in King Arthur's hall. Now he is a child playing ball, but one day he will conquer all of you. Now, good day, Dame Guenevere and Sir Gawain. I no longer have time to warn you but must wander on my way through this most desolate woods to my doleful dwelling place. But for the sake of Him who died on the cross and rose again, consider where I now have to live. In my name, feed those who are hungry and remember me in masses and prayers, for these are medicines for those who are lost, and sweeter than any spice."

And with this grim farewell the spirit floated away, still moaning as it vanished among the trees. Immediately the winds ceased, the cloud that had hidden the sky opened up, and the sun shone through brightly. The King blew his bugle and waited on a grassy meadow while his companions gathered together. The whole group rode to the Queen, each addressing her graciously. But all wondered about the strange happenings.

II

The knights, now in bright clothes, Dame Guenevere, all of them, traveled to Randalholme to their supper. Here the King was served in the hall under a dais of silk, honored, regal in his splendour. There was wine to choose, fowls baked in bread until they were a bright gold.

Just then two messengers, one plucking a citole, another with a cymbal, and following them a beautiful lady riding and leading a mounted knight. She rode up to the high dais, greeted King Arthur ceremoniously.

"Ruler, matchless in power, here is a wandering knight. Receive him courteously, as befits your reputation." The King was sitting in his mantle, his robe, trimmed with fur, preciously decorated with loveknots and topaz. He looked at the comely girl, his eyes gray and large, his beard the color of beaver, the most handsome lord sitting on a throne that anyone had ever seen.

"Welcome, lovely one," said the King. "Your knight shall have anything reasonable. Where did this attractive knight come from, if you will tell me?"

She was the loveliest girl that any man could wish for. Her gown was elegant and radiant, a grassy green. Her white cloak was embroidered with colorful birds and the buttons, gold coins both decorative and useful. Her hair was enclosed in a fine net of precious stones and bound in a filet. She wore a coronet of crystal and bright gold over a finely woven kerchief with several elaborate brooches. Everyone praised her attire and the two of them, the beautiful girl and the handsome knight, dazzled the eyes of the court.

The knight himself was magnificently armored with a flowing crest on his helmet. The breast plate and his helm had been buffed until they glittered, especially the borders of gold. The chain mail was white as milk and carefully linked. His horse was beautifully armored and glittered like a golden star.

His shield hanging from his shoulder was brilliant silver, and the arms on it, black boars' heads, were fierce and challenging. Even his metal gloves seeded

with deep red rubies gleamed like live coals. His leg
armor was polished smooth so any blow would glance
off of it, the knee plates powdered with yellow chryso-
lite. With his lance erect, he moved his Frisian mount
ahead of the lady, a squire following behind. The horse
shied, not used to seeing a decorated table in front of
him or the celebrations.

"What do you wish, young man?" Arthur asked
from his dais on hearing what the young lady had said.
"If it is your will, tell me what it is you seek. Where are
you going? And why do you remain so quiet on your
steed?" The knight lifted up the vantail of his helmet so
his face could be seen, and with a serious mein he
spoke:

"Whether you are king or emperor, I call on you
here to find me a warrior who will satisfy me in the
joust. I traveled from home to seek opponents."

"Dismount and remain the night," the King replied. "As you are courteous, tell me your name."

"My name is Sir Galeron, I tell you truthfully, and
I come from Galloway, known for its woods and glens.
But also I am from Cumnock, and Cunninghame and
Kyle, Lomond and Lennox and the hills of Lothian. All
these places you have unjustly taken in battle and
awarded to Gawain. And that fact pains my heart. But
he shall wring his hands and curse the day it happened.
He rules these lands against my will. For all the gold in
the world, he shall never rule them while I carry my
head on my neck, unless he wins them in a fair fight on
the field of battle with his spear and shield. I pledge
myself to fight any freeborn man in the world. To lose
such sovereignty is degrading, and any woman would
laugh me to scorn."

"We were here in the forest to hunt the deer with
our horn and hounds," said the King, "but we are cele-
brating now and have nothing planned. So you shall be

challenged by midday tomorrow. Take my advice, eager knight, and rest for the night."

Sir Gawain escorted him out of the hall to a pavilion of linen decorated in purple with tapestries, cushions, and magnificent hangings. Inside was a chapel, a chamber, and a large hall. A charcoal stove had its own chimney to warm the knight. His horse was led to his stall and the racks filled to the top with hay.

In the pavilion they set up boards and cloths for dining and ordered the cover, napkins, and salt-cellars, torches, candlesticks, and standards between. They served the knight, his squire, and lady with the most tasty food in silver services, all carefully prepared. They offered him wines in glasses as well as cups, and meats cooked in a special glaze. And in this way Sir Gawain delighted his guests.

When Sir Galeron had gone to rest, the King called his knights together in council.

"Look to it, lordlings," he said, "that our reputation is not lost. Choose among yourselves who shall fight with this knight."

"He will not disturb us," Gawain said then. "Here is my hand, I promise you. By your leave, my lord, I shall fight with the knight in defense of my rights."

"I rather think you do not take this seriously enough," said the King. "I do not want you to risk your life even for my crown."

"Think no more on it," Sir Gawain replied. "God stands by the right. If this knight escapes without injury, it will be a foul disgrace."

At dawn the champions were prepared. They heard matins and mass early in the day. Then the lists were prepared in Plumpton Park on the low lands, the arena and stands, an area where knights had never fought before. Bread soaked in wine was offered Gawain twice to comfort his thoughts. Then the King commanded that the son of the Earl of Kent act as squire to him.

In his pavilion Sir Galeron dined from the best of dishes, birds breaded and roasted until they were crisp. After he went to Queen Guenevere and fittingly left his own squire in her care. Then the knights brought their horses, and at the lists they mounted ceremoniously. The King's chair was set above in an enclosed box, and all the knights saluted him and Sir Gawain.

Sir Gawain was armored in green with golden griffins carefully engraved entwined with trefoils and loveknots. Both he and Sir Galeron decorated their steeds with harnesses all of shining gold. The lords led them into the lists accompanied by many sergeants-at-arms, as was customary. The fighters spurred their mounts until the sides bled. Each warrior set his spear and splintered the shafts into bits against the other's shield. Then they cut at the chain mail with their flashing swords. In this way the knights attacked one another. In one exchange Sir Gawain, his mount excited, missed his stroke. His opponent turned and called angrily:

"Why do you retreat in such disorder?" He swung at Sir Gawain's neck, and the blow was to bother him until he died. The blows of Sir Galeron were fearsome, you can well believe. Fifty links of Sir Gawain's mail, and even more, the sword cleft in two as it broke the corner of the shield and hit the collar bone. The sword penetrated a half foot or more, and Galeron's lady cheered aloud from her high seat. Gawain was angry and groaned sorely.

"I shall reward you for that blow, if I know anything about fighting," he said. With renewed spirit he charged the knight, rising in his stirrups. Sir Gawain struck with his sword. It was not an easy blow but cut right through the polished shield and the mail, and there was blood on his biting blade. Now Galeron knew fear, and his true love in the pavilion cried out when she saw the shining blood. But the lords and ladies of the castle were pleased with the blow and thanked God for Gawain's safety.

Insanely Sir Galeron lunged at Sir Gawain, and the path of the battler's weapon struck off the head of Sir Gawain's horse, which collapsed immediately to the ground. Gawain was in despair as he fell out of the saddle.

"Oh, Grisselle is dead, as God knows," Gawain said. "He was the strongest mount anyone ever bred. By Him born in Bethlehem to be our deliverance, I shall revenge you today, if it is the last thing I do. Now bring me my black Frisian, the best in the stable. He will take your place in this fight and do well, too. You, my beautiful gray, have no more life now than a dead grass root." As he stood by his dead steed that had been so faithful, Sir Gawain was nearly overcome and lamented sorely. Then he said, "I must mourn no longer for the dumb beast but must saddle the Frisian."

Then he turned to repay the wounded knight for what had happened. But his opponent withdrew some distance in fear of him, keeping an expanse of grass between himself and Sir Gawain.

"You can take all day doing this," Gawain remarked, "for already the sun has passed midday and more." Within the lists Sir Galeron then alighted, and the two warriors advanced toward each other, swords in their hands ready to battle. On foot they were like two starved lions over a kill. The shields were dented, and the mail shiny with blood. They battled so fiercely, they frightened the knights observing them. Still they wielded their swords skillfully. You well know that Sir Gawain did not lack any urging. He lunged with his weapon and under Galeron's shield. The mail did not stop the force of the blow. The sword pierced his stomach, a severe wound. Galeron staggered, then stood as rigid as stone. Though shocked and battered, he still could deliver a blow. He struck at the vantail on Gawain's helm, and at the chain pisan that covered the neck and shoulders. Gawain just escaped being killed by the breadth of a hair.

The warriors now beat on each other's helm. The shields were interlaced with fine gold which was ruined. They knocked out the jewels decorating the borders, and all the stones were scattered over the ground. The fastenings on the steel plate were sheared away. The fighters had suffered so with the blows they had received, they cursed the time they had made their challenge.

The two combatants were so closely matched in their skill neither one bested the other by right or cause, as everyone could see. Guenevere, tears in her eyes, then cried out in worry that Sir Gawain had been wounded so horribly. But this courageous knight was rugged and skillful. With his sharp brand he cut at the other right through the side of the mail. With that blow Gawain taught him painfully. Struck, Galeron fell forward on the grass, moaning.

As wounded as he was, still he forced himself up and went at his foe. Swinging his sword high in his left hand, he struck at Sir Gawain. But Sir Galeron got the worst of it, I am glad to say. Galeron attempted another stroke that would have slain Gawain, but the sword glanced off the helm and slid down the mail. And the knight hung on to Sir Gawain's neck. Sir Galeron's lady in the pavilion cried out to Guenevere fearfully:

"Oh, lady, matchless in courtesy, please now have mercy on that knight who has suffered so pitifully, if it be your will." Guenevere went over to the King, doffed her coronet, and knelt before him.

"You, the most royal and wealthiest in lands, and I, your wife, wedded of my own free will, know the knights in the battle, bleeding on the grass, are exhausted and severely hurt. Behind their shields, their bodies are torn. The moans of Sir Gawain torment my heart and grieve me sorely. Will you not, my lord, bring the knights to accord? It would bring comfort to all that are here."

Then Sir Galeron spoke to Sir Gawain:

"I never imagined that in the world there was half so great a knight. By the Cross, I release you here from any obligation, and before this King I yield my rights to you. After, I freely will do homage to you, as the man in the whole world who has no equal in his strength." Then kneeling, he addressed the King in the pavilion and offered him his sword, once so bright and clean.

"I release my lands and riches to you," he said. The King arose and commanded peace between them. And for the King's sake, Gawain ended the fight.

Other lords left their seats and leaped into the lists, Sir Yvain Fitzurien, Sir Erec Fitzlake, all energetically, Sir Merrake and Sir Meneduke, who were the greatest of knights. They supported both the exhausted fighters who were hardly able to stand upright because of the blow and loss of blood. They were bruised all over from the violence of the swords and the mail was stiff and black from blood. Now the knights were reconciled, and before Arthur they raised their hands in respect.

"To Sir Gawain," said the King, "I give treasure and gold, and the land of Glamorgan, the honor of Wales. The castle of Griffin, known for its battlements, Ulster Hall in Ireland, Wayford and Waterford, walled cities both. Two baronies in Burgundy, with their towns well secure. These places are all moated around and large. I shall make you a duke and dub you with my own hands. You shall be friends with the chivalrous knight who here fought so hardily and brave. Release the rights you have over him and grant him his lands again."

"Here and now," said Sir Gawain, "I give you without any attachments, all the lands and holdings from Lockerbie to Ayre, both Cumnock and Carrick, Cunninghame and Kyle, and neither he nor his heir shall be challenged for them. Also Lother and Lemmoke, and Leveastre Isle, all their firths and woodlands, to hold freely as lord. But we hope he will linger here a while with King Arthur as host to meet at the Round Table. I shall enfief him with these lands and forests."

Then the King and Queen with all the knights traveled through the green forests to Carlisle. When they arrived, the two knights were healed by the surgeons. Arthur held the Round Table in his royal vestments, and with the Queen entertained the combatants and made them dukes the same day. Sir Galeron married his beauteous love, pleased with the gifts and rewards he received from Sir Gawain. And thus the two noblemen held each in high esteem. When Sir Galeron completely recovered his health, on the spot he became a knight of the Round Table and so remained until the end of his days.

Dame Guenevere commanded that letters be written and sent to the west to all religious houses that they should sing masses for the intention of her mother, and the priests were asked to pray a million masses for her memory. Dukes, earls, barons, and the greatest bishops throughout all England would help with the intention.

And so once more this wondrous court rode out into Inglewood Forest and returned to their hunting, such hunting as would never be forgotten. To the forests they rode, those bold and rugged knights, and these adventures took place in the time of King Arthur, as the truth is known, in Inglewood Forest at Tarn Wadling.

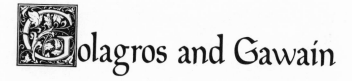

Golagros and Gawain

Introduction

The tales about Sir Gawain passed freely from storyteller to storyteller who, as we observed in the general introduction, adapted them for their own audiences. "Golagros and Gawain" and the tale following in this collection, "An Adventure of Sir Gawain," are especially interesting examples of this adaptive process. Both are related to the Old French continuation of Chrétien de Troyes' *Perceval*, started, certainly, in the last quarter of the twelfth century. Chrétien died before finishing his work, but six additions by other hands have survived. "Golagros and Gawain" was adapted, probably with at least one intermediary step, from an episode in the First Continuation, the expedition to Castle Orguellos and the defeat of *Riche Sold-*

oier, while "An Adventure of Sir Gawain" was adapted from an earlier episode in the same continuation, the siege of Brun de Branlant's castle.

Neither P. J. Ketrick, who studied "Golagros and Gawain" in its relation to the *Perceval* continuation or R. E. Bennett, who studied "An Adventure," can say that the British storyteller used Chrétien directly. If the First Continuation had not survived, we would have had no way of knowing these two tales were at one time even connected. What emerges after three hundred years between Chrétien and the British storytellers are British stories. Not only have the names of the actors been Anglicized, but the tales themselves now reflect not thirteenth-century France but fifteenth- and sixteenth-century Britain.

"Golagros and Gawain," like "The Adventures at Tarn Wadling," consists of two episodes, but the episodes in this tale are much more closely related. Both incidents of "Golagros and Gawain" are developed within the political framework of King Arthur's court, but they are not in the First Continuation. In "Golagros and Gawain," Sir Gawain always acts as an agent for the King with a specific mission, the first a peaceful one, the second warlike. Taken together the two episodes demonstrate two of Gawain's traditional virtues, his courtesy and his courage, characteristics that ideally every knight should possess.

In the first incident Arthur and the knights of the Round Table, on a pilgrimage to Jerusalem, are having trouble procuring food. Both Sir Kay and Sir Gawain attempt to buy provisions in a large, fortified city. Kay is impetuous and hotblooded and fails; Gawain is humble and courteous and succeeds.

In the second incident, the one that actually involves Golagros, Gawain fights in the name of King Arthur to establish fealty over Golagros and his castle.

Sir Kay goes out and fights on his own. Fealty, of course, is an important political concept that for about 1,200 years had been used to bind one lord to another. Arriving at Golagros' castle, Arthur is surprised, as anyone in the late Middle Ages would have been, when he learns that Golagros has been strong enough to maintain his castle free, without owing fealty to someone higher. Actually, a free castle with the land and the people it held, would have been prey to any warlike noble who wished to attack it. Golagros' speech to Gawain demanding the right of freedom is especially attractive to us today inheriting the eighteenth-century ideal of independence, but to the audience of the fifteenth or sixteenth centuries, Golagros is foolishly refusing the protection of the greatest conqueror in the world, King Arthur, not only for himself but also for the people who owned him allegiance.

The preparation to besiege the castle of Golagros is the nearest description we have in the tales to medieval warfare, but the picture stops with a list of siege weapons. The arbalest, a giant crossbow, is idealized as brass, though its decorations may have actually been brass. The stone balls mentioned as ammunition would have been suitable for a variety of catapults or for the brass cannon, now generally accepted to have been used for the first time at the siege of Crécy. In "Golagros and Gawain," the operation of the siege is reduced to a series of jousts between the knights of the Round Table and the knights of Golagros' castle.

Golagros accepts his defeat as a gift of fortune, a regular knightly attitude, but his defeat had serious implications, as his request for Gawain to feign defeat suggests. In theory, at least, fealty was only binding when a lord fulfilled his duty. In his defeat Golagros failed in his, and those who owed him allegiance had the right to dissolve the bond of fealty, now owed to

King Arthur. The bond, however, was a lifetime one and could only be severed by the death of one of the parties. Arthur would have had to kill Golagros. But Arthur, always generous in these tales, leaves Golagros and his castle still free.

"Golagros and Gawain" is known only from a tract printed in Edinburgh in 1508 and preserved in the National Library of Scotland. Early in the sixteenth century the position of the knight at court was dubious, for, as we observed in the general introduction, the importance of the knight in warfare was finished after the English longbow had defeated French knights so completely at Crécy, Poitiers, and Agincourt. The longbow and the Swiss pike restored the infantry to its place in combat for the first time since Charlemagne.

To earn a living knights were now obliged to sell their services to any lord who needed them. Even fealty was reduced to a monetary contract. At least one knight we know became a robber, Sir Thomas Malory of Newbold Rebell, probably the same Thomas Malory who wrote *Le Morte d'Arthur*. Throughout his life he was imprisoned several times for a variety of crimes: assault, rape, attempted murder, church robbing, poaching, cattle rustling.

In "Golagros and Gawain," Sir Gawain, a political knight rather than a knight adventurer, reminds the fifteenth- and sixteenth-century knight of a better ideal. The two episodes of the tale suggest that a knight still had a place in the court, that the qualities of Gawain, his traditional courtesy and courage, would make an ideal courtier-gentleman, to use a term more closely associated with the Renaissance than with the Middle Ages. We must recall that Baldesar Castiglione's famous *Book of the Courtier* was written in 1514, only six years after "Golagros and Gawain" was printed. While the story of "Golagros and Gawain" looks back to Chrétien

de Troyes and the court of King Arthur, the application
of the ideal the story embodies to politics looks forward
to the court of Elizabeth I. The tale takes the first step
on a literary bridge that ended at Spenser's *Faerie
Queene.*

This is the first stanza in Middle Scots alliterative
verse:

> In the tyme of Arthur, as trew men me tald,
> The king turnit on ane tyde towart Tuskane,
> Hym to seik our þe sey, that saiklese wes sald,
> The syre þat sendis all seill, suthly to sane,
> With banrentis, barounis, and bernis full bald,
> Biggast of bane and blude, bred in Britane.
> Thai walit out werryouris, with wapinnis to wald,
> The gayest grumys on grund, with geir þat myt
>   gane,
> Dukis and digne lordis, douchty and deir;
> Sembillit to his summovne
> Renkis of grete renovne,
> Cumly kingis with crovne,
> Of gold þat wes cleir.

The Tale

In the time of Arthur, as honest men told me, the King once went over the sea toward Tuscany to seek Him who, innocent, was sold, the Lord who gives us all our joy, truly. With him were nobles and barons and rugged knights, the mightiest ever raised in Britain, warriors fully armored, most skillful with their weapons, and the most resolute in the world. Dukes and worthy lords, strong and beloved, assembled at Arthur's call, all soldiers of great renown, magnificent kings in their golden crowns.

So the King, mighty and rich, with his Round Table moved out in royal array. Never in the world, except in lies and fables, was there a finer gathering of the flower of knighthood in one place, powerful and determined men mounted on their steeds. Many a stern warrior took to the road, banners glittering in the sun, silver and black, others gold and vermillion, still more silver and blue, a brilliant column joyfully riding over the fair meadows and glades.

But many days passed before the King found food or fire, only deep valleys, one after the other, hills and dales, mountains and morasses and many rank quag-mires, groves of birches, swamps and springs, without decent shelter, no barns or sheds. The rocks and narrow paths were harrowing even in the telling. So terribly damp was the way that they became worn and fatigued, for even the best men can tire, as you may well know. All their food was gone that once they had in great plenty, nor could they find shelter, which might have given them relief.

As they walked by the side of a clear spring, they saw a city shining in the sun, towers and turrets too many to count, huge battlements around it with high walls. The gates were carefully defended by a castle, so no one could take it by force. Only birds could fly over it.

"I suggest we send a messenger to that city," said King Arthur, still sharp and fierce, "and ask the lord who rules these lands if we might enter his town, by leave of his great renown, to buy ourselves provisions with the payment of money."

"Grant, my lord, that I undertake this mission," Sir Kay asked the ruler. "And I shall bring you tidings here, if you will wait."

"Since it seems to be your wish to go, man, be careful," Arthur replied. "See that you act wisely, and may Christ keep you out of trouble." The knight set out happily for the city, found the gates open and rushed right in. He tied his horse to a tree, then went into a large hall beautifully painted and decorated with tapestries. The rich canopy of the dais was skillfully embroidered with portraits of the greatest warriors of their day, interlaced with bright golden letters relating their deeds to everyone who read them.

But Sir Kay saw no living person, neither lord nor servant, you may believe. He went into another room also regally decorated, skillfully built, rich and glorious. He looked quickly around him and saw the charcoal in the chimney was still glowing, burning warmly. A dwarf was scampering about and small birds were roasting on a spit. Sir Kay rushed up to the fire and grabbed one of the birds from the boy, who was holding it lightly in his hand. Kay tore the wing off and was glad to eat the tasty flesh.

The dwarf yelled out, enraged, and the hall filled with his roaring. Into the hall a fierce knight strode wrathfully and stood in front of Kay. He was staunch and huge, his expression terrifying. That man would countenance no wrong toward anyone born of woman and castigated Sir Kay:

"It seems to me you eat villainously, by my faith. Your armor seems as bright as a squire's ought to be. But your manners are loathsome, according to my judgment. Why have you hurt my man? Just to show you are superior? You will pay for that rudeness, by Mary the mild. You will regret what you did, do not worry, and before you leave this castle." Kay was sudden, hot-blooded, and strong willed. He answered immediately.

"I will make little amends for anything. Your great judgment is not worth a crumb to me, and you can believe that!" Hearing what Sir Kay said, the knight swung at him angrily with his fist and knocked him right to the floor. Kay was so overpowered by the force of the blow that he lay there like a stone. The knight did nothing more but disappeared. Sir Kay pushed himself up and sneaked out the door. Then he ran hard through the great hall, out to his horse, and sped away across the moor. Exhausted, he said to King Arthur:

"Lord, go away. The lord of that castle denies your boon scornfully. To request anything further will not help at all."

"Sir, you know that Sir Kay is crabbed by nature," Sir Gawain spoke, always gracious and courteous. "I suggest you send out another man somewhat humbler in manner, who will try to be fair, and he will find friendship there. Your people are weak and harrowed for lack of food. Let us wait in the linden wood here for a better word."

"Sir Gawain," said the King, "prepare yourself for that trip, by the Cross. No one is as careful a person keeping his anger in check." At Arthur's request the valiant knight went to the town. The gate was thrown wide open and Gawain could ride directly in. He reined his spirited palfrey, alighted, and followed the same way into the royal hall as did Kay. The master was there surrounded by his knights and the beautiful ladies of the court. Gawain approached the lord and saluted politely.

"I am sent to you with a charge from noble King Arthur, courteous and generous. He appeals for his sake to your honor that he might come to this town freely to buy victuals, as dear as people will sell, paying the price asked."

"I wish no victuals be sold to your lord," the sovereign of the hall replied.

"If that is how you wish it," said worthy Gawain,

"it is reasonable since you are lord of your own possessions."

"Give attention now to why I tell you this," the lord immediately answered again, "and pass the message across that field. Everything in my domain is at King Arthur's disposal however long he wishes to lodge or tarry here. If I were to sell him what is his own while he is here, it would be wrong. I should be worthy to be drawn naked through the land.

"Earlier a crude lad came to this place with a golden belt, and other light array. By his appearance he might have been a knight, but he was angry in his manner and flighty in his conduct. I don't know why he came here, but he showed an extraordinary bad temper as if he wanted to make war. Yet I do not know who he was, by God's grace. But if it happens that he is one of your knights, he has greatly displeased my lord. I say that directly, right in his presence, and I tell you certainly, we are set against him, as I am a true knight." Gawain took his leave, returned to his steed and carried the welcome message to the bold Arthur.

"He greets you well, Lord, that great one, and it pleases him that you relieve your fatigue in his land. All the men and possessions he controls in this country, and all that he has shall wholly be at your will." Then happily Gawain led them over the long meadow to the city. The lord of the castle, his nobles, and stately ladies went to the gate to meet Arthur and escorted him in with a cheerful welcome. They led the gracious King to the high hall now filled with dukes and worthy lords all famous for their deeds.

"You are welcome, gracious monarch," said the hardy knight. "And while it pleases you to stay in this land, I acknowledge you are my master over the knights and possessions I rule in this place. There is no ruler traveling this way so dearly welcome, have no fear. I am a kindred of yours, I want to reveal. Receive this land, with its streams, forests, and valleys as your own as long as you wish to dwell here. I can reinforce you with warriors to fight, if that is your need. With 30,000 trustworthy and skillful, all in armor with mail, plate, and swords, all well mounted."

"Such friendship I hold precious," King Arthur himself replied, "one that is sustained with deeds. I will repay such kindness on my word as a knight." They all went to the benches around the tables, this King with his crown, these best of warriors, the dukes, striking to behold, each bearing his banner and each befriending the guests.

And everyone in the hall was served with all the greatest food that could be obtained from east to west and the choicest wines in cups of bright gold brightly shined. It is difficult to relate accurately the courses that were set there. The merriest were honored with food at the meal, with the minstrels joyfully making them glad. Thus they enjoyed themselves four days at an end. The King thanked his gracious host, took his leave, and went on his way.

Refreshed now with an abundance of food and wine, King Arthur and everyone with him including the knights of the Round Table and the nine greatest warriors in the land, packed their tents and returned to hunting deer in the valleys and the downs. When the day was done and the darkness of night arrived, they raised their tents again, but now they were far from the city. And in this manner these chivalrous knights journeyed each day vigorously riding over the mountains, over the hills, and through the forests. And so they continued on their pilgrimage, and the King, tested by his experiences, demonstrated his worth.

Along the way they became aware of a castle with a double moat surrounded by a wall and built on a great rock above a river. The land around was pleasant and broad and deserved the word "lovely." The sun shone bright and clear. The King examined the wall, a formidable one indeed. On the river he saw a line of substantial towers, thirty-three of them in a row. The river passing them flowed swiftly and evenly to the sea. Sixty-seven ships each with its own cargo sailed by the walls to a far country, and nothing under the heavens would impede their journey going and coming.

"This is one of the loveliest sights, I have seen," the King announced strongly. "If any knight can tell me who is the lord of this land, so fruitful and pleasing, or under whom he holds it, I would be glad to know it."

"The lord who holds this land holds it under fief to no one," Sir Spinagros said to the King, "and without allegiance both during his own lifetime and that of his ancestors before him."

"Heavenly God," said noble Arthur, "how did this ever happen? Even the most learned sage never heard of a situation so unusual. Unless I lose my life or am laid low fulfilling my pilgrimage to the city of Christ, this lord will give homage and submission when I return. I make my vow to it."

"Ah, my lord, spare us this kind of speech until you inquire more about it," Sir Spinagros replied. "This lord will not be subjected to any man except by the greatest force. You will not move that stubborn man. Many knights will be lost, their lives gone, trying it. I suggest no more vain enterprises, for the sake of God's dear son. If you believe you will scare that knight with threats, then you will leave here with nothing but scorn. It is good to be a friend and ally to the person most celebrated before your time, this great King of Macedone, most worthy and handsome. Even with his great lineage, though, he never received nor gave homage. The man who makes war whenever he thinks best, for all his worldly power, for all his wealth, he is as unstable as the leaf of the linden floating down in the breeze. Exercise your power and your kingdom with moderation."

"In faith," replied Arthur, "and you can well believe it, I shall hold to this pledge if it ends in misery or in joy. I shall never sleep except laced in my armor until I force this man to yield or until many widows will weep in anger. I have made my vow." No one dared debate with the King when they saw he had so made up his mind.

From now on Arthur rode without stop toward the city of Christ over the great salt flood. He made his offering at Jerusalem with great honor and returned home in the same way he went. There was no easing of spurs that trip, and the side of the mounts bled from the effort.

The King and his followers continued without rest, brooking no delay even when they crossed the high mountains to the Rhone River. Here on a level plain they erected a royal pavilion with golden ropes. Great ensigns of silk had brightly colored borders of gold, beaten thin. Fringes of silk were carefully embroidered with valuable diamonds one after the other. Here the king in his robes and crown called his knights and dukes together.

"I counsel now among us how best we can besiege the castle of Golagros." A warrior knight, brave and skilled, answered:

"I suggest you send a messenger to that lord, who is held in so high esteem as the proudest in robes, wise, noble, and most valiant. If that brave one will do what you wish and be bound to your rule, then receive him with honor, according to reason. But if he refuses your request, then you will be forced to besiege his castle with bold and resolute soldiers in a most perilous fight." Spirited Sir Gawain, with his high rank, Sir Lancelot du

Lake, and courteous Sir Ywain were charged by the King as envoys to the high chieftain.

"Lordlings," Spinagros said, "I suggest you give your attention to what I have to advise, for better than you, I know that hardy warrior, his land, his title, his way of life. And you three as a group are often successful in fights. But if all your strength were in one person and that person were in his clutches, he would overcome him. He is that powerful. At the same time in his manner he is humble as a maiden and as cheerful and obedient as a young bride in her wedding room. His face is like a spring flower. Yet he is stalwart and strong, and he fights well in battle.

"Therefore, speak humbly to him. Do not menace him with threats. Go about what you do with moderation. Entreat him, and act as if he were a friend, as if you would receive his favor. It never does any harm to be courteous. He is a royal lord, and a true sovereign in his hall, a man honored throughout this world."

"This counsel is valuable," said the knights, "thoughtful and courteous, and we are pleased to hear what you have to teach us."

Sir Gawain, Sir Lancelot, and Sir Ywain, well accoutred, went on their way to the castle. When they arrived, they sent a message to the lord that three knights had come from Arthur's court, and immediately the portals were unlocked for them. They continued through the castle on foot, and soon reached the round stronghold where they were met by beautiful ladies and thirty-three knights who were courteous and polite. Noble in bearing, they bowed to the envoys and were cheerful, pleasant, and ceremonious in talking the knights' arms.

The envoys went swiftly to the great hall where the lord awaited impressively. They saluted the sovereign all at once, courteously bowing and kneeling on one knee. Three more gracious persons could hardly be found. The sovereign saluted them in turn, bowing himself, his head uncovered except for a hood. Then Sir Gawain spoke, the knight gracious and skilled, always joyous and courteous, handsome and noble, and chivalrous. Nothing marred his reputation. He was eager and enterprising, daring and enjoying great love. It was he who delivered the message to Sir Golagros:

"Our sovereign, Arthur, greets you honorably," he said. "He has made us three his mediators to carry his message. He is the greatest king, revered by all who hold land, and powerful. There is no one alive his equal in majesty, none in these days so valorous in deed. Many houses, many towns, many kingdoms owe him allegiance, and his followers are more numerous than bees. He has great castles with deep moats. You would be astonished to hear the seventh part of them. Twelve crowned kings are pledged to him, who will assist him with all their great power when he needs them, plus additional warriors skilled in arms.

"Trust well that he has been told of your deeds, your worth, and your valor. Your goodness and nobility have spread far and near in the west. Our own gracious sovereign himself, truly, will not cease until he has secured your firm friendship. If gift or prayer were able to acquire it, then nothing will prevent my lord from offering you that gift or those riches. I am only telling the truth. It would be his greatest desire to be granted your friendship."

Then the lord of the hall replied with great sincerity:

"I thank your gracious lord for his good will toward me. If before, anyone living in this land had made fealty to Arthur, I, myself, would surely consent and would seek out your lord. But all our noble family have endured in this land prosperous and free of obligation. If

I would bind myself, either in voluntary submission or because of threats, I should be hanged from a tree where I could be seen waving in the wind. Keeping my followers from subjection and my titles free and without allegiance, beyond that I am able to do anything else for your king and shall take all pains and pleasure to accomplish it. In body and strength I am obedient and ready to honor him without yielding to threat. However, neither because of his sovereignty, his command, nor from fear what he may threaten, will I bow my head to any man born of woman. While I have the power to rule, I will hold to my freedom as my ancestors have done before me."

The three ambassadors of Arthur took their leave and brought him the message. So they prepared to besiege these hostile people, as always the strongest and manliest on the earth are able to do.

Noise and activity continued without interruption. Many men arrived at the city from over the sea. They immediately arranged boatmen on the moat with all kinds of weapons for the siege: the arbalest, great bows of brass, heavy stone balls, and heavy brass cannon, crossbows with quarrels, all of which would do great damage, I know. They cut down trees to make long bows and high palisades, and they groaned under the weight of the huge trees. In this way they prepared to attack the defenders, who were now angry. The trumpet blew raucous and loud, and the King flew his ensign, its field spotted gold and red on green, blazing and radiant. The shields reflected the sun brightly as crystal.

On a certain day a little past midmorning Sir Golagros and the defenders, men powerful and noble, arranged their sentries; seven score shields King Arthur's men could see at a glance, and a helm with each shield, men ready for battle with their lances up straight, bristling in the light. In this way the warriors, strong and fierce, were prepared to defend themselves against their foes. Each of Arthur's knights recognized the armorial devices clearly, as if names were written there, and they knew what man bore the device wherever he went.

"There is the best fortified castle I have ever known in all this wide world," said the wise King. "And the strongest walls, and sheer, with plenty of equipment and men undaunted, ready to withstand our attack. The castle is so high it will protect them completely. Yet I shall give them trouble and not let up. I shall win their lands with our fierce blows. They will have something new to busy themselves with for the next nine years, and I shall make my residence here in Golagros' own presence unless he defends himself forcefully and moves me from here with his own strength."

"What need is there to talk of such matters," said Spinagros, "or any terms laid down? For there are men in that castle who will account for seven deaths apiece before they are wounded. I warn you all, there are none in the world firmer in their hearts. Before they are daunted by fear, they will sooner die. They are an even match for anyone under Heaven. We will find them fierce and skilled in fighting. Sir, now you are secure and confident in your might and strength. Yet within these three days you will realize the certain truth, what kind of men they are and how they dare fight."

As the King and the knights of the Round Table were thinking about what Sir Spinagros said, the King heard the call of a bugle, loud and penetrating, just as the sun sank to its rest. A man went to the watchtower and surveyed one of the castle towers. He saw a man armed completely equipped for war carrying a steel helm and shield, gripping a spear as he moved away from the tower.

"What does all that tell us," asked King Arthur, "the shield, the helm, the spear, or the loud blast that assaulted our ears?"

"I shall tell the truth," Sir Spinagros answered him. "Yonder is a young man of Golagros' forces, a youthful and vigorous warrior. He wants to see that his lord will be safe in the attack, and because of his love, he thinks he will test his own prowess, and in your presence ride out to win fame. For this reason, order a man to challenge him in the field, one known for toughness, who can deliver strong blows, and who will fight for mastery with his spear and his shield."

The King was glad to do this and called Sir Gaudifeir, who at one time held some baronies in Britain. Cheerfully, Sir Gaudifeir went and prepared for battle. He choose all his war gear, careful to be sure he lacked nothing. His horse was berry brown, spirited, and heavy.

By midday all was prepared. Both Gaudifeir and Galiot, the warrior from the castle, were ready on their puissant steeds with their lances, long and sturdy. They could win on any field of battle. Grimly they trotted out, restraining their anxious horses. Their brilliant armor shone like a steel sword glowing in the smithy's coals. They crashed together fiercely, and with drawn swords hewed at one another bashing the hard steel, bruising the flesh beneath it. The force of their blows penetrated right through mail and plate, as you well know.

They fought murderously on that field coughing up blood. They battled over an area of a mile or more, fighting vehemently, as if they were insane. Both of the knights, sore and wearied, remained right in the thick of it. In a fresh onslaught Gaudifeir and Galiot fought so deadly, they both fell to the ground. Gaudifeir arose again first, with the help of God, and overcame Galiot with the effort he had remaining. King Arthur and his knights praised God and St. Ann.

Galiot was carried into the castle, and Golagros became angry. He called for Sir Rigal of Rhone, a bold fighter.

"I shall never rest until this fight is revenged in that field and with the weapons of battle. On a war horse that is strong and quick, I pray you, for my sake make the fight a costly one for them. Never before was my heart so troubled." The warrior left and prepared his gear. With a customary blast on the horn, he picked up his shield, helm, and spear. King Arthur knew well what was occurring in the castle and called Sir Rannald, a tough and keen warrior.

"If anyone is coming here to test our prowess, prepare yourself in your best armor to meet that knight." Sir Rannald took pains to obey that command by sunrise. His mail and light basinet helm were shined, his spear sharpened, and both his horse and his armor decorated in the same colors, gold and crimson trimmed with green. His bright, gleaming shield carried the sign of three boar heads, as his family had before him when they were in Britain.

When morning arrived and the sun was shining brightly, a knight rode out of the castle ready in his steel. It was Sir Rigal. Sir Rannald loped out on his mount. Both settled their lances in the rests, ready and stern on their two coursers. The two warriors collided and their lances splintered, completely disintegrating against the shields, pieces flying over the heads of the men and onto the ground. The horses were staggered by the clash and fell over, the two fighters landing on the ground. Continuing the combat on foot, they drew out their swords and hacked at one another making

flashes and sparks on the steel plate. Sir Rannald lunged
fiercely at his opponent, and catching him at the shoulder in a wide wound, cut through fifty links or more.
The blood flowed out on the ground around them so
everyone watching could see it and gasped sorrowfully.
Immediately both warriors fell over. Though both had
been rugged, apparently both their hearts burst with
the effort. All who were watching were confounded by
the cruel fight. With great mourning and sorrow Sir
Rannald's body was brought into one of the tents, and
Sir Rigal was taken into the castle. The contest ended
honorably, and people have remembered both knights
for their hardiness. Both of their bodies were buried
within a hour, and masses and chants were set for their
souls.

Then Sir Golagros prepared four men in their armor: Sir Louys, the true, with the rank of a lord; another
called Edmond, who had proved a great lover; the third
Sir Bantellas, a leader in battle; the fourth was a skilled
warrior named Sir Sanguel, handsome and savage.
These four went into the fight. Sir Lyonel with his spear
was paired against Sir Louys; Sir Ywain against Sir Edmond, both equal; Sir Bedwar against Sir Bantellas to
take his chance; both were considered excellent under
pressure. To Sir Sanguel, good Gyrmolance was paired.

It was in this arrangement that these famous
knights met in tourney with a great clash. Golagros'
knights, without allegiance to anyone, glittering in their
shields, set upon the other. The sturdy warriors, their
weapons sharp, rode their cruel courses, charging
forcefully. Their horse strained, held first in check, and
when the men released them, they jumped like sparks
from flint. The knights splintered their lances and fell
to the ground, but this did not stop them at all. They
went right to battle with their swords. They struck their
shining armor with heavy blows as rapid as they were

powerful. The mighty warriors fought their courses royally. They hacked the hauberks so boldly they loosened the links of mail and burst them like hail. Their shoulders were injured, and in spite of their shields, their blood flowed over their armor. The men groaned aloud in their exertions.

The King cried out worried about his knights, who though fierce and strong, in that contest tested their powers incredibly. The melée was so great that no one could judge which of the knights was better than another. Only God, who rules all, would be able to judge. The warriors gave each other terrible bruises and shocks, wounding each other with their battle swords. They battered and hewed their steel helms doing themselves terrible harm in the exchanges. They punctured their byrnies with piercing thrusts then drew out their daggers, and each man, bloodthirsty against the other, penetrated the armor at the joints mutilating the other.

Sir Louys took Sir Lyonel in hand, and Gyrmolance captured Sanguel. Sir Ywain laid Sir Edmond out on the ground and brought him to grief, weltering in his own blood. Sir Bedwar yielded his sword to Sir Bantellas, and in that battle those strong fighters were brought to a standstill. None of the great men who were fighting escaped without mauling or a wound, though they had been equal in the melée. But none of the vanquished was proud of what happened. Bedwar and Lyonel were led into the castle, and the handsome Sanguel was led back to Arthur. Sir Edmond lost his life, and the most famous of the knights carried his body to the castle tenderly. Sir Ywain received injuries dreadful and sore.

Before another day dawned five more knights, who had gone to the tourney, prepared for their fight. They were spirited as wild boars and said, "We shall even the score or die for our pains." They laced on their helms, their mail, and their breast plates, and made ready all their necessary gear.

Sir Agalus, Sir Ewmond, honorable and skilled, Sir Mychin and Sir Meligor, both men of great estates, and with them Sir Hew, hard and eager, all went out of Golagros' castle. Now I will tell you the fighters of the Round Table who had prepared themselves to handle the new challenge. Wondrous to regard, they rode out when the trumpets called them. Sir Cador of Cornwall, handsome and famous, Sir Owales and Sir Iwell, Sir Myreot, and mighty Emell would ride to the fight.

No truce existed between them, you may well believe, when these mighty ones clashed. They spurred their mounts bloodily, cradled their lances, and riding the courses, emptied the saddles immediately. Then with their swords they beat on the armor, attacking so hard they seemed to draw sparks like fire from flint. Their weapons cracked the armor in the force of revenge. It is harrowing to recount even a tenth part of their brutal strife, they fought so murderously. Sir Owales and Iwell were both captured and were taken to the castle together, their part in the battled ended. Both Sir Agalus and Sir Hew were led to King Arthur. Then Sir Golagros' eyes were tearful in grieving, but, too, he was angry as the wind and wrung his hands.

"I shall bring a different end of this," he said still undaunted. "Tomorrow I will take the field myself, in truth." He went to the belfry and rang two small bells.

"What does that ringing mean?" royal Arthur asked.

"I shall tell you that truly," Spinagros answered him. "The man who rules that castle, let me warn you without question, believes that he alone can fight for his cause. No one has proved his equal in strength. You would do well to choose a fighter who will stand up skillfully against him. He is the strongest man alive and fortune is his friend."

Sir Gawain asked that he might take up this challenge. The King granted it to him and prayed to God, our Sovereign all powerful, maker of men, that He keep Gawain safe and uninjured. Sir Spinagros was sorrowful and mourned deeply for Sir Gawain.

"For the sake of One who was slain without reason, do not take that knight as an opponent in this difficult encounter. No one is as stalwart in battle and can hold his ground so stubbornly as that king, Golagros. And I grieve the more that you should accept this deadly encounter. Since you are so respected, skilled in battle, greatest in renown, most valiant in deeds, will you not refuse the battle with this knight, even if all the wealth in the world is offered you as reward?"

"If I die valiantly, the less is my loss," Gawain answered. "Though he were Samson himself, as Christ is my guide, I will not pass this fight by for all his accomplishments. You would be well to understand that, without doubt."

"Since unquestionably you will fight this battle," Sir Spinagros replied, "take this advice. It will be worth your while if you put it into practice. When you match him on the ground, run at him squarely and carry your lance to the middle of his shield. And hit him savagely, for the love of Christ in Heaven. Then do as I advise in handling your weapons. When that stern knight is surprised, he shouts loudly, but he becomes as rough and fierce as a wild boar trapped without cover. Do not let what he does annoy you.

"Even suppose his blows dent your shield, do not become careless in what you do. That will cause you harm. Let the great man rage and fight courageously swinging his sword until he tires. Afterward you will get in your blows. When he is exhausted, then strike and keep him moving. In this way you will surprise him even if he is strong. You can be confident in the outcome through the advice I teach you. Unless you fight wisely, you will be defeated and will deserve it."

At the break of day the King and his knights prepared Gawain in his armor which was customary. But Sir Kay was unhappy, as you might know, because he was not chosen for the fight. He went and readied his gear, rode right toward the castle, and stopped in a hidden valley. As he waited, a knight came along riding a brown steed and armed for battle. He was dressed in a mail byrnie and an excellent basinet helmet. He gave his battle cry and engaged Sir Kay immediately. They ran a single course, violent and keen. Both of them hit with their lances and both were knocked down. On the green earth they took out their swords and without delay hewed vigorously at the steel plate. Between them was a rough reckoning. They scattered the links of the mail over the grass, and their blood ran through the byrnie, and over the breast plate like roses on a shaggy bush. Each received terrible injuries. The knight then complained to Sir Kay of his hurts.

"I suggest we stop this heavy fighting," he said. "I will yield you my sword since there is no better way. When fortune fails a man, no effort is worth it." He lifted the visor of his helm.

Kay was glad to receive that sword, for he was bruised, mauled, and bleeding. Though he was weakened, he could still act mercifully, and sincerely wanted no harm to come to his opponent. Both went to the King leaving their lances behind.

"Lord, if you will listen, no harm will befall you," Kay said. "Have no misgivings in your heart. Often I have read in romances, 'Early haste is slow speed.'" Then he led the knight to the King's pavilion. They removed his armor so they could treat his wounds, and the leeches were not too late with their healing salves.

Then many people accompanying Golagros in his magnificent equipment came to the field. He was armed in red gold and large rubies and with many ancient, royal decorations. As he walked on the ground, he wore finely embroidered silk. Sixty great warriors, clad in brilliant armor, perfectly equipped, arrived on prancing steeds harnessed from withers to croup. Golagros himself rode on a horse of pure white, his harness decorated completely with gold and jewels. To describe his armor would be a great delight, but it would be difficult to relate all the preparations that went into it.

His reputation and nobility could not be denied. No knight there was as tall as he by half a foot. He pranced his mount over the land without stopping at the list where he was to prove his strength. By this time Sir Gawain himself was prepared in his armor and arrived at one side of the field waiting for the battle to commence, ready to ride with his shield and his spear.

The two fighting knights left their friends at the fence of the list and faced each other alone. Immediately they made two charges, each warrior against his adversary to test him. They urged their two great horses until they whinnied in anticipation. Then the stones resounded with the hooves when the knights collided together. Their helms smashed to pieces, their lances splintered, and the mounts were completely staggered by the clash. Each knight turned back so rough was the collision. No one could see weakness on either side. The knights sprang from their horses and quickly drew out their swords hewing at the hard steel with terrible fierceness, for both had hearts noble and strong.

Golagros' anger against Gawain increased, and he slugged at his plate. With all his power he swung at the mail pisan around Gawain's neck and burst more than fifty links of the chain. Gawain was staggered with the blow and for a moment was shocked, the blow was that strong. But recovered, Gawain lunged at his foe with his sharp and burly sword, which had often been his safety and protection. He went at the man with all his anger and hacked off one of the upper corners of the shield. The blow continued through the breast plate and mail. The gold leaf that decorated the plate fell to the ground. The edge of the sword drew blood along its route in spite of the armor, right through the golden clasps and rivets. He dealt such blows that Golagros was headed for danger and fright. The jewels on his armor hopped off to the ground.

King Arthur offered a prayer to Christ. "Lord, as Thou lent us our life here on earth, and as Thou made all fruit for our sustenance, give me comfort today as Thou art truly God." In this way the fearful King prayed for Sir Gawain.

Golagros was as angry as a lion deprived of his food, and with both his hands he swung his sword smashing off mail and plate. Knights watching yelled anxiously in fear that Gawain might be vanquished. Golagros sheared through his armor and lopped pieces of his shield more than twenty paces from him. Sir Gawain was startled and now fought impulsively and madly.

He struck at Golagros repeatedly, bashing him with his sword. He chopped at the plate with all his strength going for the helm through the gems and fastenings. He hewed off half a span at a blow and so tore up the armor.

Golagros jerked back, then hit Gawain beating down on his breast plate and slicing some of it away. Gawain was shaken by the blow and was not able to fight coolly. The jewels on his arm piece, emeralds, rubies, and sapphires, sprinkled on the ground. Both fought on grimly, both fought in anger, Gawain and Golagros lashing at one another, hammering and slamming. Again King Arthur, knight, squire, and child all sought the help of Jesus:

"As Thou art truly sovereign and master, grant that

Thou wouldst protect Sir Gawain, and grant that he be superior, though save the honor of both of them."

Determinedly and maliciously the knights fought on. They injured each other through the mail, and each brought havoc to the other, slugging without care or direction, the armor running blood. Then, as Golagros leaned forward, his feet gave way, and he fell flat to the ground. Before he could rise again, Gawain seized him, happy at the turn of events and thanking Christ that his heart was strong. Gawain took out his dagger and addressed the knight, who had been so rugged and keen:

"If you love your life and are true to your word, give me your sword. Do as I say or beware what will happen!"

"It seems to me it would be better to die than be disgraced," the other answered him. "Never have I been vanquished or my reputation stained, nor any of my ancestors before me. But I am one who rules the kingdom and my own self regally. No man under the sun will see me humiliated, nor shall anyone, regardless of rank, say my name is discredited. I swear by the true God who made the world in seven days. If in the glory of fighting I have been conquered, I ask no favors. Do what you will, you will get no more of me today."

When from afar many of the lords and ladies of the castle saw their lord overcome, they swooned away. His worthy companion knights wrung their hands in grief. There was no solace in that castle, nor was their suffering little. A sorry confusion and chagrin took over their hearts, and they lamented to Christ:

"On the cross as Thou bought us with Thy blessed blood to bring us out of the bonds of sin, never let our sovereign end in shame. Mary, fairest of countenance, beseech thy son for this intention, to allow us one droplet of thy grace." But the knights of the Round Table were overjoyed.

Sir Gawain entreated the knight to change his wish to die, for Gawain was unhappy to cause him more harm.

"Sir, for yourself you see you are vanquished," he said. "It cannot change that fact one jot to make it so difficult. Arise and go to our King. Living under our law, you will lack nothing including a noble rank, even to being a duke."

"It would be foolish to make a profit at the expense of my honor," Golagros answered, "for I would be ashamed all my life. Shame is the reward the man receives who loves life more than earthly honor. No one, neither friend nor foe, learned or ignorant, shall force me to hide myself from my people. No wise man will disparage the fate of one who leaves this world honorably. In spite of your plea, let me tell you in just a few words, I will not alter my intent for all this broad world. I will not give up a penny worth of honor for rich trifles. Understanding the choice, I do not fear to die." Sir Gawain pitied the royal knight.

"How can I help you at all," he said, "and not impair your honor in the presence of all these people?"

"I shall tell you," replied Golagros. "If you will subject yourself to my plan, then let me bestow the honor on you as I wish. Right now, let me have the honor as if I had overcome you in this battle. Then come to my castle, which is my chief concern. In this way you may save me from disgrace. On my word as a Christian, I shall repay your kindness and preserve my own reputation."

"This is difficult," said the noble Gawain, "on my life, it is a perilous idea involving great danger to trust in your honor and rank without proof of it. I never saw you before. I am trusting in your fidelity, but if you were disloyal, I have put many brave knights in jeopardy. But I know you are brave and fierce. Before you are doomed to die, I place myself in your trust, by God so beloved."

He leaned on his sword, and Golagros quickly rose up. A knight never received such a grace from his opponent. Then the two combatants carried out what they agreed. They fought again but now feigning. They drew two short swords from their scabbards and duelled over an area of a mile or so. No one, not even the King, knew of their agreement, for it seemed by the appearance that their anger was aroused again. Afterward they effected their treaty. They put up their swords, and both Golagros and Gawain went to the castle, Gawain as if he had yielded and was taken prisoner. King Arthur seeing this was mournful. He cried out in wrath, pitifully. He was inconsolable. His warriors saw the tears run down his cheeks as if everything he had in the world had been taken away. Others blackened their faces in their grief.

"The flower of knighthood has been captured by Golagros," they said. "Now the Round Table is rebuffed in spite of its lands and wealth when Sir Gawain, who had won such respect, is led into prison. Now our fortune has turned from good to bad." The King wept long.

When Sir Gawain, the gracious knight, had come to the castle, the people there were joyous and happy over the victory. The men and women praised their lord, Golagros, and were blissful and jubilant. But the knights of Arthur's court were downcast, and the joy on one side was the grief on the other.

Within the castle, when the knights sat at their supper tables, Golagros, the lord, was marshal of the hall. He sat Gawain at dais where only he, his wife, and daughter were seated. He placed the strangers he had captured around the table seating them according to their rank, with a beautiful lady between each one. Lord Golagros regarded them pleasantly as they were gathered at the fete. Then he announced loudly to everyone who was there:

"All you good people listen to me." He struck the table with a staff he held in his hand. No one said a word more, and everything was still. "You are gathered here together, all the greatest nobles that have possession of baronies and towns in these lands under my fief, and as the most fortunate in the world, you have a voice here. I have a request to make of you, great knights, about what happened here.

"In friendship, with neither falsehood or pretence, truly and faithfully, tell me about a matter that burdens my heart. It touches my honor closely, and I want your plain answer. I require it, and I shall conceal nothing. Give me your choice, one or the other, whether you wish me as your lord, humbled in the field, or should I give up my life and hand you over to some lord who could defend you?" When they heard what Golagros had said, the nobles were sorrowful, for now they understood that their lord had been disgraced.

"We want no sham favors here," they said, "neither to friend or to foe. We like you always as our lord, both to war and to rule. You may not give up your life. You shall be our governor in satisfaction and honor and in any chance that may occur while this hall will endure." When these courteous and humble knights answered him and told him this intent, then Sir Golagros told his followers how Gawain had beaten him in the field of combat and now had power to do with him whatever was his will. Golagros related how well Gawain had fought.

"In the full view of his own sovereign lord, the noble Gawain saved me from disgrace. It is an unforgivable sin, that a knight's honor should be lost. He gave me this courtesy, and that is the greatest he could show.

As a prince I ought to praise him for his skills that, although he won the day, still he did not lessen my reputation. Now I am ready at his bidding and glad to obey him who ended my misery. I make his great kindness known, so I may do him an equal kindness if I am able." He rushed over to Sir Gawain. "Sir, by conquest I know you are a great man," he said, "when both my life and my death you had at your will. I discovered your friendship, freely given. Now I will obey you. I give you my hand in homage, as is right and proper. Because Fortune guides events through her cunning, I did what I had to do, not out of fear, weakness of heart, or cowardice. Where Christ guides events, they run easily, and nowhere can any strength or power test His. But when Fortune turns the wheel, then all grace passes a man by. He who can endure defeat and scorn the destiny that makes him faint at heart, cannot endure his fate any longer than God decrees. Any man knows this by experience, be he knight, king, or emperor. My experience is a mirror of this truth.

"Hector, Alexander, and Julius Caesar, David, Joshua, and Judas Macabee, Samson, and Solomon, all who were wise and respected, or any of the greatest rulers on earth, when they meet at the appointed mark, then they can do no more to speed them over the spearfield than we can do. When fortune is hostile, prosperity fails, all treasure departs, all riches and honor leave. In spite of whatever Fortune means by her tricks, either good or ill, everyone gets the reward he deserves by his work and his desires. Sir Owales and Sir Iwell, gracious and hardy, Sir Lyonel, Sir Bedwar, too, and Sir Gawain, that brave knight, courageous and worthy, I return to the King. I, myself, shall go out with you, for my lands and my castle are his as part of the victory."

The royal company was quickly arrayed, all the lords and ladies, beautiful to look at. They carried bril-

liant lights, bearing sixty torches before Sir Golagros. It
was a magnificent sight. King Arthur, however, was
frightened of what was happening and thought that
Golagros approached for another fight. His warriors
took their lances and formed a skirmish line, preparing
themselves across the road in their heavy armor.

"Do nothing more," Sir Spinagros said. "They seek
a reconciliation, I see by their appearance. They are
approaching in rich clothing. We have done our duty
without any doubt. I know our worthy Sir Gawain is
responsible for what is taking place. Friendly glances
pass between him and Golagros, I observe, and other
knights have a peaceful demeanor."

Sir Golagros went up to the King with his sixty
knights, all in their most courtly dress, impressive barons around him, and the lords in clothes of bright gold.
They bowed low to King Arthur and saluted his retain-
ers. Courteously the King took Golagros up by the hand.
Then Golagros spoke:

"At this time I come here into your presence, the
most revered king in the world, worthy and wise, the
richest in lands of all the rulers in the world, for
strength, unsurpassed in renown. Here I make you a
promise always to offer you all my service. Wherever
you go by the sea or by land I shall be ready at your will
with all my reason and strength. And I shall hold to this,
in truth." Then he told Arthur and his nobles the reason
for this promise, how he was beaten in the fight by Sir
Gawain and what happened afterward.

"This is a kingly thing, by Jesus, I think," Arthur
himself replied, "to trust yourself in such peril and in
such great danger. There was great hazard had any one
of you injured the other. But since your loyalty has
proven true, then your accepting my kindness makes
you the more worthy. And I thank the great knight.
This makes me happier than if I had all the lands and

wealth from here to Roncesvalles and had taken them into my own hands."

"Because of that bold man, who released me from bonds," Golagros immediately answered, "all that I possess under Heaven, I hold in fief from you, from the sea to the hills and the forests, wherever they may be. Since worthy Gawain has won the right of governing for you, goodly conqueror and king, here I make obeisance to you as my liege and lord of my holdings. And since I make firm homage to you without reservation, and so that event may be recognized from my actions, I bow and am obedient to you, and I must acknowledge this." King Arthur was happy with Sir Golagros and thought the agreement was right. It was fulfilled in friendship. At his own request Sir Gawain had King Arthur escorted to the castle to inspect it with all who were there, knights, barons, earls, the twelve peers, both lords and bachelors.

The sovereign was received in the great hall at a tremendous banquet. An abundant selection of wines came from the cellars for each warrior at his place. It would be impossible to enumerate the details of them. The knights sported over a whole week and followed the hounds through the forests along the Rhone River. On the ninth day, the visitors took their way home with no delay.

And when this renowned monarch with all his worthy followers were assembled to ride out, the King, decked with his crown, said to Golagros:

"Here I give you a reward, as I have reason to, before all these great lords, concerning the estates and castles, and towns, by the sea, the mountains, and the forests, large and small. I release you from your allegiance. But certainly I shall warrant you, you are as free as I first found you, without any argument."

An Adventure

of Sir Gawain

Introduction

"An Adventure of Sir Gawain" is the second story with a parallel in the Continuation of Chrétien de Troyes' *Perceval*. What results here in the course of transmission is something quite different from what happened in "Golagros and Gawain." As we saw, the events of the Continuation are adapted in "Golagros and Gawain" for a didactic purpose. The qualities of Sir Gawain, his courtesy and his courage, exist not for their own sake but as instruments of Arthur's policy and as ideals for sixteenth-century knights. In "Golagros and Gawain," we have what might be called a political romance.

In "Adventure" two aspects of Sir Gawain's reputation, Sir Gawain as lover and Sir Gawain as warrior, are illustrated but apparently for their own sakes. We would not like to believe the tale suggests an ideal of conduct. If "Adventure" has a larger purpose, it cannot be discerned, especially since the beginning of this English version has been lost.

In the episode of the French Continuation Sir Gawain has been wounded at the siege of Brun de Branlant's castle. Before he fully recovers, he rides out to try his strength, and in a spring woods his wound is miraculously improved by the fine weather and the singing of the birds. Riding along he discovers a pavilion occupied by a maiden on a bed. As soon as she is convinced her visitor is truly Sir Gawain, she promptly surrenders. Later departing Gawain promises to return to her, but on his way back to the besieged castle, he has to fight the girl's father, brother, and finally Sir Brandelis, who agrees to postpone the fight until later, because Gawain is suffering from his old wound. In a second version of the same story in the Continuation, Gawain does meet Brandelis and is defeated by him.

Judging from the first surviving sentence of the English "Adventure," the siege has not been used. Gawain is hunting, a common beginning for a tale as we have seen. Gawain has also received some sort of threat from the girl. Possibly she has warned him about her brothers, as later she warns him about Sir Brandles.

"Adventure," like the "Green Knight," is another example of a tale adapted for a popular audience. The story has been reduced to its essentials, the seduction and the four challenges. Even transitions have been omitted that, reading silently, we think necessary, as for example, the necessity of Gawain's putting on his armor when his lovemaking is interrupted. The transitions, though, would be less apparent when the tale is delivered verbally.

Although the "Green Knight" is preserved in the

most famous manuscript of popular ballads, there are more elements in "Adventure" that have characteristics of the ballad. The "Green Knight" is a much more complicated story. Here the repetition of the four fights, the use of dialogue, the elimination of unnecessary detail are suggestive of these same qualities in ballads like "Edward," "Lord Randall," "Barbara Allen," or "The Wife of Usher's Well." Still, "Adventure" is not a ballad, if only because it lacks typical ballad refrains. However, if the development from courtly romance to ballad were an evolutionary one, "Adventure" might be considered a link between the two.

Only in this English version is the seduced girl beaten by her brother and left to wander far and wide. In English medieval tales, love outside of marriage is usually severely punished. Chaucer's *Troilus and Criseyde* comes to mind and, especially, Robert Henryson's *The Testament of Cresseid,* where Cresseid becomes a leper as punishment for her sins. The element of adultery in courtly love or *fine amour* was not as congenial to the British audience.

In relating this particular episode, the storyteller gives it an ironic turn, for the girl, warning Sir Gawain about her brother, has obvious pride in him. We know nothing else about their relationship, however. The complicated emotions of this episode are left unexpressed, an understatement also typical of ballad narration. The incident of the beating also reflects the position of women during the Middle Ages more accurately than those stories written in the tradition of courtly love.

The title of this story in Sir Frederic Madden's collection *Syr Gawayne* is "The Jeaste of Syr Gawayne." *Jeaste* is one of the spellings of the Middle English word *gest* defined in the *Middle English Dictionary* as "a poem or song about heroic deeds, a chivalric romance," or in a second meaning, "a noteworthy deed or event, a heroic action." The word developed in two directions, one ending as our modern word, "gesture," the other as "jest," a joke. For the title of the story here there seemed no way to use *gest* without suggesting "jest," so we abandoned this family of words completely.

The tale is preserved in a uniquely illustrated manuscript of the Bodleian Library, Oxford, Douce 261. The dialect in which it is written is not that of Northern England but Southern and South Midlands of the late fifteenth century. The verse is not alliterative, but, as can be observed from these lines of the original, it is rhymed in quatrains.

> And sayde, "I drede no threte;
> I haue founde youe here in my chase,"
> And in hys armes he gan her brace,
> With kyssynge of mowthes sweete.
> There Syr Gawayne made such chere,
> That greate frendeshyp he founde there,
> With that fayre lady so gaye;
> Suche chere he made, and suche semblaunce,
> That longed to loue he had her countenaunce,
> With oute any more delaye.

The Tale

"I fear no threat," Sir Gawain said. "I found you here while I was hunting." He embraced her in his arms and their sweet mouths kissed. The welcome that Sir Gawain received there in that pavilion from that gamesome lady developed into an affection, and without further delay her friendliness and charm aroused lovemaking between them.

He had not been with her long, however, when a

knight, tall and strong, entered the pavilion and found them together.

"Sir knight," he said, "what you are doing is evil and will disgrace you. It is my daughter you are lying with. You have been a villain, and there is no way you can make up for it. You have had good fortune with that lady. The familiarities you have taken with her were never before given to any man because of her modesty. For what you have done I can see that Fortune is your friend. You had best lace on your armor in a hurry. You have greatly dishonored me and that cannot be recompensed, by Mary. So dress yourself quickly."

"I suppose I have this maiden's love," Gawain answered, "for I have found her gracious. Since you are her dear father, sir, I will make amends here. As I am pledged to knighthood, I will fulfill anything I agree to and will make amends to you. So let me be excused."

"No," said the older knight, "it would be contemptible unless we first test our strength to the limit of our ability."

"I grant you that," Gawain said, "since it will not be otherwise. What will be, will be."

He took his strong horse by the bridle and leapt lightly into the saddle like a good and royal knight. Holding his great spear he took his horse out a large furlong then turned it around. Both cradled their spears and rushed together eagerly, there on the mountain where the pavilion was. Gawain hit the other knight so hard he overthrew him, horse and all, and he lay on the ground face up. Sir Gawain turned his horse toward the fallen man.

"Sir knight," he said, "do you want any more?"

"No," he said, for he would not be able to take any more. "I yield myself, sir knight, into your hands, for you are too strong for me to stand against. But grant me my life."

"On this guarantee," Sir Gawain said, "if you do no harm to the girl, I will agree to your request. Also, you shall swear on my sword here that you shall bear no arms against me either today or tonight. And then take your horse and go your way, and I shall do the best I can, as I am a true knight." The knight swore to that and paused. He was called Sir Gilbert, a rich earl, strong in battle.

"Sir knight," he said, "take good care, for you will be more strongly assailed by many a sharp attack before you sleep tonight."

"I can well believe that," Gawain said. "When they come, then you will hear how that game will go. Now I am enjoying myself here, and I will not go away for any threats that I may be more sorry."

Sir Gilbert then went his way. His horse had wandered down into the valley below, and he had to go along on foot. Without saying anything more, he went down. Sir Gawain had hit him on the shoulder, and the strokes had grieved him sorely. His pride had diminished. After he had been walking a little while, the wound started bleeding again, and he rested under a tree. He had been there only a short time when one of his sons, Sir Gyamoure, arrived.

"Father," he asked, "what ails you? Has any man in this forest hurt you? It seems that you are bleeding excessively."

"Yes, son," he replied, "by God's anger. A knight has shamed me, and I have lost my horse. Also he has lain by your sister, by the cross of Christ. That grieves me more than the blood I have shed. And the injury is still more. He made me swear that I shall bear no arms against him, by the glory of God."

"Father, be of good cheer. As I am a true knight, I will give him his reward, and you will hear about it. I will beat him to his death in spite of how fierce he is."

"Let it be, son Gyamoure, I pray you. You say more than you can do, and that you will know soon. Before your journey will be over, you will meet with a strong knight who will give a good account of himself."

"Now farewell, father," Gyamoure said. As fast as he could, he made his way to his sister at the pavilion where Gawain and she still lay together, no argument about that.

"Get up," Sir Gyamoure said, "you strong knight, and give me battle here on this ground. And right now; move quickly. You have hurt my father today and lain with my sister, and you have earned your death."

"If that is so," Gawain answered, "I will make amends before I leave, provided I have done anything amiss. It is better now to be in agreement than that we should fight. So go away from me."

"No," said Sir Gyamoure, "that will never be. You will never see the time, knight, that I allow such disgrace. Get up immediately, for I wish to fight with you alone, as God gave me life."

Gawain saw no way around it. His horse was close by, and he sprang buoyantly into the saddle grabbing his spear in his hand. He was eager. Each took his horse about a furlong away, I dare say, then charged, spurring the horses until the sides were red. What do I need to say more? Gawain hit him with his spear so firmly that he fell flat on the ground, and his horse ran off still excited. The knight was hurt where he lay.

"Sir knight, do you wish any more?" Sir Gawain asked him as he lay there.

"No," he said. "I am so badly hurt I cannot move. I yield, sir knight, and save my life, for I do not want any more fighting with you. You have won the field."

"Sir," Gawain answered, "I grant you this covenant, that you promise me to bear no arms against me today. Swear to this on my bright sword."

"Yes," he said, "as I am a true knight, I swear that I will not harm you today. Now farewell, knight, and may God heal me. I see Fortune is your great friend. That she showed today. There would be no reason in jousting again, for you are a powerful knight. Farewell, and have a good day."

So wearily on foot Gyamoure went down from the mountain, and his father soon spied him.

"Oh welcome, my son, Gyamoure," he said. "It seems to me you have not succeeded well in this battle. I can see that clear enough. You went up the mountain on horseback, but now you are woefully on foot. This is why I am disquieted."

"Father, it cannot be anything else," he said. "That knight up there has beaten me in fighting and has badly wounded me. Actually," Gyamoure continued, "I will not lie. He is a strong knight, daring and bold. I believe he is of King Arthur's court, I suppose a member of the Round Table. When necessary he is both tough and able. That is how I have found him, with no exception." While they were speaking, a second brother, Sir Terry, rode along on a spirited courser with a pace like wild fire. This knight had a good reputation, and his heart was full of pride. He was not aware of his family, but his brother called him over.

"Wait a minute, sir!" The lively knight turned his horse with a leap. He found his father all bloody and his brother wounded sorely, and he was sick at heart.

"Oh, sir, who has wounded you?" he asked. "I want to be avenged on him, and that won't please him at all."

"Truly son, it is a strong knight up there on the mountain," said his father, "who has done us this wrong. He has wounded me severely, indeed, and I believe your brother well may have more wounds, and he has lain by your sister. Therefore, go now quickly as a good knight should and avenge the shedding of your father's blood. See that you do not fail because of any cowardice, but meet him with all the force possible, for he is good at riding tilt."

"Father, I can see well he is a strong knight. But he has done you a great wrong. It will be hard to conquer him, but, nevertheless, I shall do everything I can. I would test his strength in a fight were he the devil's kin."

Sir Terry turned his horse and rode up the mountain as fast as his horse would go. He came proudly to the pavilion.

"Have done with it, sir knight," he called out, "and mount your horse, for I have a quarrel with you." Sir Gawain looked out of the pavilion door and saw this armed knight in front of him.

"Sir, if I have offended you in any way," he said to him, "I am ready to make amends, by our mild mother, Mary."

"No, sir knight," Sir Terry replied, "that cannot be. Therefore make yourself ready fast, in all the haste you can muster, for you can make no reconciliation. So now let us go to it." Gawain saw there was no other way. He took his horse as he should and with great abandon jumped into the saddle.

"Now, sir knight," he said, "let us have done whatever you mean in your heart to do."

"See, here I am," said Sir Terry, "and I have a great hatred for you." They rushed together with a terrible force and a strident crash. Gawain rode hard on that course. He pierced Sir Terry through the shoulder and threw him over the back of his horse. His helm hit the ground so hard he was nearly killed.

"Sir knight," Gawain said from the height of his saddle, "do you want to fight any more?"

"No," he answered. "I am hurt so badly I cannot

stand up any more. I yield you my hand and pray you mercy."

"What," said Sir Gawain, "is this your great boast? I thought you would have fought until you sweated. Is your fight all done?"

"Yes sir, in faith, may God save me. You cannot have any more of me. My strength is all gone. Today you have honorably defeated three knights, my father and his two sons, who all fight well. And if you can defeat our eldest brother, I will call you the best knight that ever fought under a shield, and no other. He is all warrior, I warn you well, and will last better than steel. And that you shall soon see. If he is a match for you, I cannot know. In knighthood you have no equal, I assure you, on my faith."

"Now," said Sir Gawain, "let him be. You, sir knight, swear me an oath that you leave me paid completely, that you are now satisfied and will reproach me no more."

"I grant that," Sir Terry said. "Farewell now, and God protect you." He left weakly on foot but did not rest until he came to the place where his father and Gyamoure were, who had troubled hearts, God knows.

"Sir, you got what we got, and nothing different," his youngest brother, Gyamoure, then said. "I well knew that's what would happen."

"By God," said Sir Terry, "so it did now. He is a devil, truly. He proved that to me."

"Yes," said Sir Gilbert, the old earl, "he is a knight strong and bold with Fortune his friend. He has won my daughter's love completely, and for that I say he is a man, no devil, whatever he might be." As the three of them stood talking, they heard someone singing so loud that all the woods rang with the song.

"That is my son, Sir Brandles, in good spirits," said

Sir Gilbert. "When he sees the trouble we have, he will leave off his song." By then they saw the knight riding a good mount and carrying a green bough in his hand. His horse was decorated in red velvet set with many jewels, and the head and chest of his horse armed in good steel. He, himself, was armored in harness that had proved it would really resist hard blows well. His helm was decorated with a shiny boss.

His horse leapt around. His shield was well known, silver with a black falcon. In his hand he carried a spear of the best wood, strong and long, I would like to tell you, and with the hardest steel as a head. It was the best that could be bought or made and had been well tried in battle. From it a kerchief hung more than three ells long embroidered all with gold. He wore spurs of gold and carried a sword that would bite to the bone. He was a big knight and tall, and anyone who had tested him knew he had great strength.

"Alas, there is some bad news here," he said when he saw his father all bloody and his two brothers unquestionably wounded. "Alas, who has done you such a disgrace. Tell me, quickly, that I may repay it, for my heart is filled with sorrow."

"Son, I will tell you," said his father. "A cruel knight who has also lain by your sister. He beat me first and all of your brothers. And he made us swear that we would not do him any harm today."

"This is an evil mishap," Brandles said. "I assure you on my oath, I will test his might. If he were as strong as Samson, in faith, I will never leave him until one of us is dead."

"No, son Brandles," said his father, "that should not be. Though he has done wrong, let him go. This knight is of surpassing power. More than anything else, Sir Brandles, I do not want to see you slain there, for I warrant you, he will stand firm. The knight is strong, can fight well, and when he faces an opponent, he can ward off hurt. Be temperate in your speech to him, and he will be temperate in his actions to you. Don't try to use physical strength to harm him."

"Do not say any more about him," said Brandles. "Soon we shall see if he is man or devil." Then saying, "Have a good day," he rode straight to the pavilion. When he arrived, the girl saw that it was her brother.

"Sir knight," she said to Gawain, "a knight comes now who will be hard to overcome. Look and see. Here comes one who will last through a fight. I'll guarantee you never saw a better knight that you will find him to be, surely. Look at my brother, Sir Brandles. He is an expert in war, truly. And you will find it out. It seems to me he looks the way a knight should. Have no fear, you will know he is fierce, right here under these trees."

"By God," said Gawain, "A man is likely to suffer blows and knocks from his hands. For the last three years, I have not seen anyone more likely to be manly, by God and St. John!"

"Where are you, good squire?" Sir Brandles asked. "Hurry up and come out, for I am going to fight with you. You will learn a new game. You have done me a dishonor, and it is too late to make amends. This is no time to speak of peace."

"Sir, I pray you," said Sir Gawain, "before you begin this struggle, let me come to some agreement and you can as well. Sir, if I have done anything wrong, tell me, and it will be corrected immediately, to fulfill what is chivalrous. I have been sorely tested today, and it would be a shame to test me any more. Nevertheless, I will abide by your wish."

"That is true," said Brandles, "but I must needs hold to my oath to my father. You have done such wrong. You have beaten my father and my brothers, and if I came to an agreement with you in this, it would defame my honor."

"Since this is the way it is," said Sir Gawain, "I will

have to turn to it. May God give me grace today. My words have not gained me anything, so let us see how we do violence, if I can dare anything along this track."

"Thank you," said Brandles, "in good faith. Now you will see an unequaled exercise in knighthood. I am glad you are powerful but sorry we lack daylight."

These two good knights went at it. The red blood soaked through their coats of mail and it was pitiful to see. They fought so angrily that even after the flame of the sun was out, neither would let up. Finally they had no light at all and did not know what to do.

"Sir knight, we lack daylight," said Sir Brandles, "and I think that if we fight in the dark this way, one of us may slay the other by accident. Therefore, I'll agree to this. Let us both swear on our swords that whenever we meet again, in friendship or hatred, we will never leave off the battle until one of us be slain."

"I agree to that," said Sir Gawain, "if you wish it that way."

"I cannot do anything else," Sir Brandles said, "for I made such a promise to my father. Therefore we will swear this oath. I know there is no stroke you gave me that I did not repay equally, and you are not in my debt in the same way either. You deliver a hard blow, sir knight, no one else ever tested my power as well. We are as even as when we met. Let us make an oath on our swords right here, that wherever we meet, far or near, whoever finds the other, then we shall battle to the finish."

"I hold to that," said Gawain, "by Mary mild. And so make an end to this." Sir Gawain put up his sword. "Sir knight," he added, "be a friend to that noble lady as you are a noble knight."

"As for that," said Sir Brandles, "today she has caused great disgrace. It is a pity she has her sight."

"Sir knight, I must bid good day, for I have a long

way to go on foot and horses are dear. Many a time I have won good horses, but now I have none. May God quickly change my humor." Gawain took his knife and cut himself out of his heavy armor, for otherwise he could not have walked.

Now we will leave Sir Gawain still sorrowful and we will speak more of Sir Brandles. When he met his sister, he said:

"Fie on you, you sinful harlot. It is a pity you live so long. I will deal you some hard stripes." He beat her both back and side then left her and went straight back to his father.

"Son, I have been worried about you," said his father. "I thought you might be shamed."

"I have beaten my sister," Brandles said, "and I made the knight swear that when we meet again, we will fight until our strength is gone and one of us is slain."

All four of them went home together each helping the other as best he could. The lady went her way wandering far and wide, and they never saw her again.

Sir Gawain exhausted and on foot went until he came home to Arthur's court. He told the king all the adventures he experienced fighting with the four knights one following the other. After that time they never met again, and both were glad about that. And so this is the end. I pray God give us a good rest, and those who have heard this little adventure will sometime dwell high in Heaven, and that at judgment day, we may all come to everlasting bliss where we may hear the angels sing.

The Avowing of King Arthur, Sir Gawain, Sir Kay, and Baldwin of Britain

Introduction

In the Middle Ages a vow was a serious obligation. We saw how the Carl of Carlisle kept his vow for twenty years. There was never any question that Sir Gawain would keep his made to the Green Knight, and in the last story of this collection, King Arthur kept his vow to Gromer Somer Jour and to Dame Ragnell. In this tale, the vows of four knights have gathered three stories and three anecdotes into a single framework. King Arthur keeps his vow by killing the boar. Kay's defeat and Gawain's rescue of him and the beautiful girl resolve their vows, but Baldwin's vows: that he will not be suspicious of his wife, that he will feed anyone who comes to his door, that he will not fear death, have to be tested by Arthur and Kay. Having kept his vows through the tests, Sir Baldwin explains why he made them by telling three anecdotes, all related to defense of a castle in Spain he was awarded while fighting the Moors. The stories and the anecdotes are all different from one another, yet they are joined together smoothly by the framework.

With the wolf practically extinct in England, the wild boar had no enemies except the hunter, and a number of tales describe that hunt. The boar is a fearsome beast today and was even more so in the fifteenth century. Archaeological evidence indicates that it then stood four feet tall at the shoulder and weighed about 300 pounds. Its two tusks were like butcher knives, and the boar could use them to either stab or rip. Its successive layers of bristles, hide, muscle, and fat were impenetrable to arrows. To attack this beast alone with only spear and sword was exceedingly dangerous, and Arthur's vow was no mean one.

Kay's and Gawain's vows blend into a single story contrasting these two knights as usual, but their story is less noteworthy than that of Baldwin. Baldwin's name is also found among those knights with Arthur on the Continent in the alliterative *Morte Arthure,* in Sir Thomas Malory, and we recall that in "Sir Gawain and the Carl of Carlisle" he was Bishop Baldwin. In this last tale the bishop acts like a knight, but here the knight talks like a bishop. There is nothing unusual about this inconsistency, for all characters in the Arthurian stories are modified as they pass from one narrator to another, as we have seen.

Essentially, in his stories, Baldwin is using the technique of medieval sermons citing *exempla* to illustrate the virtues, two of which are generosity and courage. Generosity, as Baldwin illustrates it during the siege, was not the same generosity that the ghost of Guenevere's mother extols, though this is the generosity Baldwin practices when his vow is tested. At the siege, offering the messenger food was only a technique to raise the siege, a technique that went back to Greek military manuals.

Baldwin's third episode provides a good example of the difference between psychological cause and effect, by which we judge a story to be true today, and the cause and effect by which a story was judged to be true during the Middle Ages. Baldwin tells how two servant girls, envious of the beauty of a third, murder her. Later one of the survivors murders the other for the same reason. After each murder the survivors perform their duties in an exemplary fashion, to say the least. From this experience Baldwin learned that in an atmosphere of good will, women "become obedient and submissive."

The cause and effect of the anecdote, if judged psychologically, seems naive and shows Baldwin as unfeeling. The motivation in the anecdote, however, as it is in many medieval tales, is based on the scholastic concept of sin. The servant girls are driven by envy, one of the deadly sins. When the occasion for envy is removed, even by murder, then the girls are no longer envious, and their conduct changes quickly and completely until, again, an occasion for envy arises, it is removed, and the same change results. That the girls commit murder is secondary, a consequence of the envy. Baldwin applies the principle of the occasion for sin or the occasion for good to his own life. By providing only occasions for good, then his wife will be good, and he has no reason to be suspicious of her. Judging psychologically we accept more Baldwin's statement that he had known his wife for a long time and knew she would not be untrue to him.

The setting of the tale is in Inglewood Forest and Tarn Wadling like "The Adventures of Arthur" and

"The Marriage of Sir Gawain." Apparently the tale was also originally written in the North of England, though the single manuscript that survives shows evidence of having been copied by a scribe in the West Midlands about 1425. Each stanza consists of four quatrains, which, as will be noticed from the first stanza given here, requires three consecutive rhymes and a fourth line rhymed four times—a difficult pattern. The manuscript, The Ireland, now in Geneva, also contains a version of "The Adventures at Tarn Wadling."

> He þat made vs on þe mulde
> And fare fourmet þe folde
> Atte his will as he wold,
> The see and the sande,
> Giffe hom ioy þat wille here
> Of duȝti men and of dere
> Of haldurs þat before vs were,
> þat lifd in this londe.
> One was Arther the Kinge,
> Withowtun any letting;
> With him was mony lordinge
> Hardi of honde;
> Wice and war ofte þay were,
> Bold vndur banere,
> And wiȝte weppuns wold were,
> And stifly wold stond.

The Tale

    May He who made us on the earth, and at His own will formed the dry land, the sea, and the sand give all them joy who will hear of the brave and valiant men who lived in this land before us.

    One was Arthur the King, and with him was many a young lord strong of arm, wise and skilled, bold in the fight, ready with their weapons to stand their ground firmly. This is no fantasy or fable. You well know about the Round Table where the greatest and most worthy men were esteemed most highly. These leaders in courtesy and chivalry all hunted eagerly, brave men and skillful, riding into the forest to chase the buck, the boar, the hart, and the hare, which breed in the great thickets.

The King stopped at Carlisle, and one day a hunter came to him.

"Sir, a grim beast stalks my lands, an evil boar," he said. "I never saw such a one before. He has given me great trouble and killed my hounds in the toughest fighting. No one is so foolhardy to stay around where he is. I broke my spear and my arrows on his hide without doing him any harm at all or even wounding him. He is massive and tough. There is hardly a bull in the down that is as large. He is taller than a horse and is not without strength when he fights. He is black as a bear, and the people of the woods are frightened of him. Nothing will stop him. After he whets his tusks, he rips through bushes, running and tearing them up by the roots, rolling up great clouds of dust in his fury. Whoever can stand up to him is a man true enough. He is in Inglewood Forest."

"Do not disturb the son of Satan," said the King, "until we take a look at him, if he really exists." The King called on three knights, and he would be the fourth himself. "No one else is going after the boar," he added. They were Sir Kay, Sir Gawain, and Baldwin of Britain, the hunter and master of hounds, who prepared them for the hunt. The four of them, hardy and noble, rode into the forest. At the north end the hunter blew his bugle and loosened the tracker dogs, who knowingly raced south one after the other following the scent of the boar excitedly with their mouths open.

When the boar heard the baying, he was worried and withdrew into a cave, though surely you may know, he had little fear. The men held him fast in the cave, but when the dogs attacked, he cut them to pieces, both the experienced and inexperienced. The tracking dogs ran at him to bring him to bay, but none of them dared attack the fiend.

"Leave him there," the chief hunter called. "Don't go after him anymore. You will have a chance soon enough. Then we will see who does best. I swear on my head the grizzly devil will slay all four of you." The hunter himself returned to his home, and King Arthur spoke to Gawain, Baldwin, and Kay:

"Sirs, I make a vow in your company. That hunter was not hardy enough to attack this child of Satan, but on my own life, and by tomorrow morning without any help, I will bring him down and prepare him for the kitchen. And now, sir, I command you, do as I have done. Each of you make a vow." Gladly they agreed.

"I vow to keep watch at Tarn Wadling all night," Sir Gawain said.

"And I vow," said Kay, "to ride around this forest until day, and to bring to death anyone who challenges my way."

"So I will not be different," Baldwin said, "I vow on my life never to be suspicious of my wife or of any other pretty girl, nor to refuse food to any man, whenever I am able, nor to fear any threat of death from either king or knight."

After they made their vows, they were prepared to fulfill them, and each one went on his way. The King turned toward the boar, Gawain toward the Tarn to watch until day, and Kay, as I heard tell, rode up and down the forest. Baldwin went back to the town where his castle was and went to bed.

Let us talk about the other three and how they fulfilled their pledges, speaking of the King first, naturally, and how he accomplished his vow. He attacked the boar with his hounds, but the boar, huge in the shoulders, charged at them and routed them quickly. The King called to his dogs to give them courage and leapt on his horse. Before he set upon the King, the boar first whetted his tusks which were three feet long. Then snorting angrily, he rooted up tree trunks and rocks. As soon as the King appeared, the boar charged at him. Never had the King seen such a sight, and he was afraid of the fierce and heavy beast. The boar roared and snorted and attacked with his mouth wide open. No one knew how he charged, for previously he had killed both men and dogs, drawn them into his den and stripped them to the bones.

The King cradled his spear to hold the boar off, but the strike did not injure his thick hide. Instead the long spear splintered; the horse and the King were knocked to the ground. Before Arthur could get out of the way, the boar gave the King such a blow, he felt it the rest of his life. His horse was struck dead and never moved from the place, and the King prayed to Jesus to protect him.

King Arthur leaned against his saddle and valiantly struggled to his feet praying to St. Margaret to guard him. Then he acted like a brave knight. He drew out his bright sword, raised his shield high—of course, his spear was of no use—ready to run at the hideous fiend. When they met, for all the strength that Arthur could use, the boar still smashed his shield.

The King knelt down and prayed to Him so generous:

"Send me victory. This Satan is after me." The swine was wrathful, snorted and rolled his eyes. He smelled vile, like a hot kiln or a kitchen. Though the King could not see him, still Arthur was overcome by the stench and rested down by a tree, the smell so upset him. Then as he approached an oak, the King struck at the boar fiercely. By the look of him the King knew he was stunned, and Arthur had the upper hand. The boar had never received blows so hard. With his great sword in his hand the King met the boar's threat by charging at him. The sword entered the throat. The boar had no joy of that attack. He had received a deep injury and began to stagger and reel then sink slowly down. The King finally destroyed him, slashing him across the shoulders.

The King had learned the skill of butchering and according to the custom, cut him around the neck. He set the head of the hardy beast on a stake and prepared him like the best venison in the forest. He hung strips and slices on the oak tree and then knelt down to her who is so loving and said:

"These are for the help that you have sent me, for your son's sake." He was in a deep valley with no knight there to wait on him. Weary, he slipped into a deep sleep. Thus the King fulfilled his vow.

Now we must talk of Kay. How he exercised his skill, you shall now hear. As he rode in the forest during the night, he met a knight leading a pretty girl. She was weeping copiously.

"Holy Mary save me and save my maidenhood," she said, "and for his villainy give this knight sorrow and worry." As she said this, Kay was still and remained in the woods. Then he spurred out quickly and overtook the man yelling at him, reproving him.

"You cowardly knight. I offer to fight you here because of that young girl. I demand it on my glove."

"I am ready if you think you can fulfill your challenge in any way," the other answered him.

"Now who are you?" Kay asked. "And where are you bound? Tell me your right name and where you won that girl."

"I will not hide my name," the other answered him

again. "It is Sir Menealfe of the Mountain. That is what
my father called me. And I will tell you about this lady.
I won her at Liddle Mort, north of Carlisle. There her
friends, opponents in a fight against me, let her down.
I told them I was able to spill their blood even if they
did not want to. And I won this girl there."

"I'll do you battle for the girl's sake," said Kay. "I'll
make you suffer," and immediately he swore to it.

Then, as men do in their fights, they rode at one
another because of this pretty girl, who was beautifully
dressed. Menealfe was the stronger, and with his sharp
spear he hit Sir Kay hard, as you might well know. He
demolished his shield and knocked him out of his saddle right to the ground. So Menealfe took him as a
captive. He broke his spear, and his other equipment,
armor and weapons, Menealfe took as a prize.

"Sir, at Tarn Wadling Sir Gawain waits for me," Sir
Kay told him, "and he has a wide reputation among
knights. If you would go there before you return to
Carlisle, he will pay you an immediate ransom."

"Sir Kay," Menealfe said, "I will put up your life in
a course against that knight." Yet before it was midnight, Menealfe regretted his haste in that pledge.

They went back to the Tarn with its thorn trees.
Kay called out and Gawain asked who was there.

"It is Kay, who you know, and I made a boast I
could not keep. Unless you free me by your efforts, I
shall lose my life. For as I rode in the night, I met this
knight leading this beautiful girl weeping. Because of
her we fought, and this knight won me. He has a great
reputation and has taken me prisoner. You must pay my
ransom, Gawain, with your leave."

"I will gladly," said Gawain. "What shall I give?"

"When you are armed, take your shield and spear
and ride a course against him. That shouldn't worry
you."

"Is this so?" Gawain asked. The other knight granted it was. "Then we will ride together, whatever happens," Gawain replied.

Both of these knights knew their craft, both gripped their spears, heavy as beams. They ran at one another so close neither could escape. Even if Menealfe was heavier, still Gawain struck him sharply and immediately knocked him out. The horse that he was riding did not know which way to go.

"You have what you were after," Sir Kay called out. "My ransom is already bought. If you had been killed, I wouldn't have cared. That's why I came here." So Kay scorned his captor, but Gawain rode up to him and set him back on his saddle and let him speak if he could. He drew off Menealfe's helm and let the wind blow on him. Then Menealfe spoke in a low voice:

"You have delivered Kay. You have ransomed him in a fight. He is loath to be at peace, but you are always courteous and a prince of the joust. If you would rest here for a time, I would ride another course for this girl lying by my side. She is my wager."

"I would be glad to fight for her," Gawain answered, speaking courteously again. So the knights took their gear and with their spears ran a second course as fierce as the first. They clashed together, and Gawain carried Menealfe from his steed so he bled around the forehead when he hit on the ground.

"Sir, you have had a fall," Kay called out to him, "and you have lost this wench, I promise you. You have lost your love, for all your brag and boast. If she has cost you anything, I tell you it's paid now!"

"Good fortune does not last forever," Gawain told Kay. "No one is certain in what he does that he may not sometime be harmed." Gawain rode up to the other knight who had been hurt in the fight, but Kay's words angered Menealfe more than all the blows he endured.

"If we were alone," he said to Kay, "I would put a stop to your insults."

"That might be," said Kay, "but you have lost your fair maid and your life, I'll warrant."

"God forbid," Gawain answered, "for he is strong in fighting." He prays that the knight does not take Kay's words ill. "Ride with the girl to Guenevere the Queen," Gawain continued, "and fulfill this agreement. Tell her that Gawain, her knight, sends her this lovely maid, and she will ransom her to you as she wishes." The knight agreed to this and gave his word that he would take the girl under safe keeping to Carlisle, swearing his oath on his broad sword.

As the day began to dawn, the King awakened and blew his bugle. His knights knew it well, and immediately started off to discover what it was the King wanted. Gawain, Kay, Menealfe, and the girl took their way through the forest to the King. They found the boar all cut up by the King's hand, but, though he was King of the land, still he had no horse. So they set the girl behind Menealfe and gave her horse to King Arthur. They gave the meat to Kay, and they all went homeward to Carlisle.

As they rode along, the King himself asked Gawain and Kay:

"Where did you win this girl?"

"In the forest as I kept watch at the adventurous oak," Kay replied. "First the knight won me, but Gawain made my ransom, won this pretty girl, and took the knight prisoner." Then the damsel laughed and happily praised God and Sir Gawain.

"What is the ransom?" the King asked the knight. "Please tell me truly."

"I cannot say," the knight replied, "for it is according to the Queen's will. Why should I lie? My life or my death is at the discretion of your wife, whether she will take away my troubles or put me in pain."

"Great God!" said the King, "May Gawain always be blessed. He can be depended on tilting with a knight. He always takes the prize and wins the praise of the ladies. Menealfe, if you are wise, hold to your promise, and I shall help you all I can."

They took their way to Carlisle and alighted at the court. The knight took his gracious lady before the Queen.

"Madame, I am sent here by Gawain, your knight," he said, "for last night he won me in a joust over this lovely girl. He injured my pride, and made me swear to bring her and myself to do as you will. And I have done as he ordered."

"And I am glad," said the Queen, "since you are put in my will, to spare or to punish. I give you to the King, for he has need of such knights in the tourney. He will fulfill this agreement." Then the Queen added, "Almighty God, save Gawain, my knight, for me, who can fight this way for women."

"Madame, as God gives me success," Gawain said, "Menealfe is valorous, a good man on a horse, all ready in his gear."

Then they brought out a book to search for their laws. The King took Menealfe's oath and made him swear, absolutely, without any reservation, that he would dwell at the Round Table as a deserving and ready knight, with shield and spear, and they became good friends.

Sir Kay then spoke to the King:

"It seems to me there is something extraordinary about Baldwin's vow that he took yesterday evening, and without any hesitation. It was much more than we three took."

"That is the truth," said the King. "No longer can I hide that I would be glad to know how it might be fulfilled."

"If you would give me leave, and do not object," Kay answered, "I would test it myself as best I can."

"If you will agree to this," said the King, "that, on the pain of your life and your lands, you will do him no wrong, but keep him from harm. Accost him resolutely, and afterward bar his way. But you will not find him standing around defenseless. Be careful, for he is strong and well horsed and completely armed, and there is not one of you but he may feel he can overthrow. You will not force him out of his way. I dare mention," the King added, "that he takes great pleasure in holding to what he promises."

Six knights were of one mind in this. They armed themselves and rode out over the fields to meet Baldwin. Their weapons were sharp and ready, and over their armor they wore a gipon of green to keep their armor clean and dry. Three rode on each side so they could deny the way to Baldwin. Wherever he would ride, they would block him. They covered themselves with capes right down to their feet so they appeared as strangers. Because of the capes, they would not be recognized.

Now as they were waiting, they saw a well-favored knight on a good horse behind his shield, spurring fast over the field toward them. He was armed and eager like a man ready to fight and was riding briskly in the direction of Carlisle when he saw the six in his way.

"He's afraid now, I'll warrant," Kay said, "and worries for his life. Immediately Kay called out loudly to the knight. "Either flee or fight; you have to choose one or the other." Then they cast off their capes, and Sir Baldwin saw what Kay said was true.

"Even if you were twice as many, you would not

make me flee," said Baldwin. "I have to go my way to speak with a friend, and as you are obedient vassals, you will not stand in my way." Then the six joined together and swore:

"By Him who bought us dearly, you will never leave here unless you are dead."

"Certainly he can take another route," Kay said, "and no one who knows that will say anything about it."

"May God reward you!" said the knight. "For I am right on my way. Yesterday evening I asked the King to come to eat with me. And I warn you people, even if you are arrogant, I am going to stay on the way I have taken." He placed his heavy, long spear in its rest. Kay stood closest to him, and he knocked Kay down in his charge. Kay's large horse fell on top of him so he was pinned to the ground.

Baldwin then rode at the other five, and he was able to crack their bright shields. Four of them he felled quickly and angrily. Without delay the sixth had picked up Kay.

"Do you want any more of this?" Sir Baldwin asked him.

"You may go where you want," the knight answered, "for you have only done what was right to us, even if we are severely hurt."

Baldwin hurried over to the King without delay and the King asked if he had heard anything in the thick woods. The knight thought about it.

"Sir as I came through the wood yonder," he said, "I heard or saw only tranquility wherever I rode." The King wondered why he would not tell him any more.

As soon as they were ready they went to mass, and by the time mass was over, before noon, Kay arrived and told the King:

"We were all disgraced by Sir Baldwin, your knight. He is noble, bold, hardy and strong when he rides the field. He would never run away. He would much rather stand right there. I can curse her who bore him, for I have suffered great pains."

"He is unable to flee," the King replied, "nor deny food to any person. If any man would curse him, it would be extraordinary." Then the King called his minstrel and told him what he wanted—but ordered him to be completely quiet about it—that he should go to Baldwin of Britain.

"I command you before you return, that you stay there forty days or pay the penalty. Then let me know secretly, if any man leaves his house without being fed, and, on your honor forever, do no more than that."

While Sir Baldwin remained with the King, the minstrel took his way as fast as he was able. By noon of the third day at the gate of Baldwin's castle, he did not find a porter to refuse him entrance. He found the lady and her attendants with guests in large numbers at dinner. He made his own way into the great hall among the highranked and the low, and when he looked all around him, no one tried to restrain him. The service was royal and splendid. The squires passed around the wine in great bowls, and in the kitchen the cooks sweated and scurried.

The minstrel bowed to the ladies and young girls everywhere and could find no fault within or without. Knight, squire, yeoman, or servant, none of them lacked anything. They only needed to wish for something, and it was given them.

Then he went up to the dais before those who had the highest reputations. Here the hostess was courteous and asked him to remain. He said he was known and respected, and had come from the south country. She was happy to hear his news from his own mouth.

He remained at Baldwin's castle a week and no expense was spared. The tables were never bare but always completely covered with food. Both knight and squire, minstrel and messenger, pilgrim and palmer were welcome with plenty of food. The poor had their needs fulfilled, both food and drink, before they left, I say without contradiction.

Lord Baldwin did not remain long with Arthur but, as was his wish, returned and brought the King and Queen with him. Now the royal and splendid service was supplied from the kitchen. There was no lack of wine both to those of the highest rank and the lowest. At their supper they had the most expensive foods. The King with a joyous manner bade them banish care, and from the dais he addressed the knight without hesitation.

"I never saw such a service," he said. Sir Baldwin smiled at him and laughed.

"Sir, God has a good plow," he said. "And He can send us all enough. Why should we be sparing?"

"Now I command you," the King said, "that tomorrow in the morning you go out hunting to win us a deer. Go out to the fens and take men and hounds with you. Which are the best here, you know well. For all day tomorrow I will ride no further but will wait here with the great ladies for their good cheer." They went to bed that night, and at daylight in the morning the horns sounded and Baldwin went out with his companions.

Then the King called to his hunter.

"Fellow, come here." He came cheerfully and knelt before the King. "I command you to be out all night. Baldwin, who is hard and strong, shall be with you. Early at dawn make certain you return from the hunt. If you do not bring any venison, that will not worry me at all."

"Sir, that is as you wish it," the hunter answered him," "and I regard it reasonable and right, as God prospers me."

That evening the King arranged things and called a knight to him. Immediately they went to the chamber where the lady of the house and her ladies in waiting, who were gracious and attentive, were actually in bed. The King ordered:

"Open up!"

"Why?" the lady asked.

"I have come here for some secret fun," he said.

"Don't you have your own queen here?" she asked. "And I have my own lord for my lover. You won't get any closer to me tonight, if I have my way about it."

"Undo the door," said the King, "and in the name of Him who made all things, no harm will come to you except as you wish it." One of the girls arose and let in the King. He sat down on the foot of her bed and talked to her.

"Madame, my knight must lie with you all night until daylight tomorrow. Do not get upset about it. For as God prospers me, you will not be harmed. We do it for a bet to settle an argument." Then the King said to his knight, "Get undressed quickly, and get into that bed right away." The knight did as the King ordered, but when the Queen saw him naked, she became fearful. The shrewd King, still dressed, said, "Lie down right beside her, but do not get any closer to that lady, for if you do, you will die because of your wicked deed. Don't be so forward as to even stir or once turn toward her."

"No, sir," said the other, for he feared the King. Then the King called for a chess board and for one of the girls. They sat down together at the side of the bed. Many torches were lit and lamps were burning brightly. But that knight was not so bold as to even hide his head once. But from the time that the others began their chess game until the day dawned, he waited for Baldwin just as he had lain down.

And early in the sunrise Sir Baldwin and the rest returned from the hunt bringing harts and bucks home to the kitchen, of which they were proud. The King sent after Baldwin and asked him to come see what was happening. Baldwin took his way to the chamber and found the King playing chess and a knight lying in bed with his lady.

"I missed my knight," the King then said, "and I followed right after him and found him here. And I held them both here, so you could do with them what you wish. And if you are now disturbed about this, I would not think it strange." Then the King asked, "Are you angry?"

"No, sir," Baldwin said, "and I do not have to swear to it. Nor do I wish my lady any harm. I will tell you why. For this was at her own will, or else no person would dare come near her. And if I am disturbed about this, then I really have to be angry. We have been together many winters, and yet she never did me any injury. Each sin must first be proved and judged severely then."

"I had wondered why you were not angry," the King said, "when you found that your lady brought him to bed."

"If you will stay," said Baldwin, "I shall do my best to tell you."

"Yes," said the King, "and I order that you keep nothing hidden."

"It happened during the time of your father," said Baldwin, "that King Constantine gathered together a large and excellent host and went into Spain. We warred against the Sultan and, before we stopped, conquered him and his lands and were pleased about it. I was so admired by the King that he put obedient and willing nobles under my leadership to do my bidding. He gave me a castle to guard with lordship over it. I had five hundred and more people at my meals, but no more than three women among them, who were our servants.

One of them was more beautiful than the other two. Two of them agreed that they would have the third seized. They went into a spring house and said to her:

" 'Since you are the most famous, you shall lose your reputation." And as fools do, they immediately slew her.

"We were disturbed by what they did and threatened to slay them.

" 'Let us have our lives, and we shall do as much of what you order as all three of us did,' one of them said. 'None of you privately shall lack a wife.' They fulfilled their promise well during the day and during the night they served us well without complaint. But one of them was lovelier, and the other envied her and secretly cut her throat with a knife. We had much difficulty deciding what we might best do. They asked my counsel if we should kill her.

" 'No,' I answered. 'Let's find out first what she will say, whether to atone she could serve us all. That is a better idea.' In the great hall she promised us to do all the work that would fall to a woman, and to serve well all of us who stood in the hall. And what she promised she fulfilled well. During the day she did her work for us, and during the night she offered her body for us.

"And by this tale I learn that women when they are humble and when they devote themselves to a good life, will greatly mend their ways. But when they give themselves to an evil life, they commit their foolishness. Then reason tells me there will be no love in them. Quickly, completely without threats, with good will, at home they are obedient and submissive, and they bring joy in every way. Therefore, I shall never be suspicious because of anything I see or because of any beautiful woman. Anything here on earth comes to an end in any case."

"You speak well," said the King. "Sir," he added,

"as God gives me happiness, I want you to know just what happened, and that is the reason I am here. Your lady implored me to swear before I could enter that neither she nor her company would be harmed. Then I ordered my knight to go into bed with the lovely girl, on the right side where the light is, and lie down by her. I sat down beside them to wait for you there. He did not approach the naked side of your lady.

"Therefore you may be certain you need have no suspicion. You have held to your vow. But I wish to know more of the other vows you made me. Why do you not fear your own death or that of anyone who eats your bread? As far as I know, the gates of your castle are always open."

"I shall tell you," said Baldwin. "At the same castle where this adventure occurred, we were besieged. One day we rushed out to take prisoners for ransom. One of our fellows was worried and was afraid to go out with us. The clod crept into a barrel that was set out in the sun. A projectile from a catapult came glittering like lightning and hit the barrel. It broke it all apart into six or seven pieces, and it slew him there also, he whose heart was so false. His head was completely severed from his body. We returned from the fighting sound, with no wounds, and we praised the King who is in the highest Heaven.

"From what happened, our companions could say that no one will die before his day unless he throws himself away for lack of sense. And there I made my vow and so did all that company, never to fear death, for it is welcome; it is something natural."

"You tell the truth," said the King. "But of the third vow, tell me what the reason of that is, why you will never deny food to any living person."

"True, no man will lack food, Lord," said Baldwin, "you shall well know. For when the siege was all around us, we did not have enough food or drink to satisfy us. We lacked all sustenance. Then a messenger came and ordered, 'Give over everything that you have!' I did not reply harshly, by the Cross. I ordered him to wait until noon. Then I called the steward and told him what he should do, according to a good plan. He blew the trumpet on the wall, and covered all the tables in the hall, and I stood among them as king.

"I made them wash and come to meal. Then I sent after the steward. I ordered that he should see we all eat well. I ordered him to bring plenty of bread and wine in wooden bowls. There should be no lack for the highest or the lowest. We had food for no more than a day. It came in nobly served. The messenger kept looking and saw us put cares aside. He took his leave from the meal. We made him drink at the gate and gave him splendid gifts when he went his way. But when the messenger was gone, each one of the officers complained drearily to me, I can tell you.

" 'There is no food in this house,' they said, 'neither white nor red wine. You had best give this place up and pray for our loves.' But God always helps His own.

"The messenger then returned to his chieftain and said:

" 'Though this siege has gone on for seven years, you will never take this castle, for they make merry as if it were Yule. I counsel you,' the messenger continued, 'leave this place immediately, for there is no joy in your army, only hunger and thirst.' Then the King called to his knights and they went into council.

" 'Because nothing better will come along, I hold this best, that we leave this place.' Right at midnight, their lords, who were strong and hardy, assembled in plain sight, leaving their beds. They had concealed their own lack of food, and our food broke the terrible siege and made them turn their backs on us so they were pressed to ride out.

"And we looked where they were and saw our enemies had gone.

" 'He that receives a benefit and still deprives people of food, let God, who is great, give him misery. For the food given to the messenger rid us of all our worries.' "

So that all could hear, King Arthur said to Sir Baldwin immediately swearing an oath:

"There is no falsehood in you. Your vows are beneficial."

And this is recorded by the Round Table, the highest and the lowest. Then the King and all his knights celebrated in the hall, and they called that lady the fairest man could embrace.

"Baldwin," the King said, "if you are wise, you will take this esteemed lady, for a deep love lies within her. Hold her to your heart. She is a beautiful girl and attractive to your sight, and you have fulfilled all that you promised, as a knight should."

Now Jesus Lord, Heaven's King, grant us all His blessing, and give us all a good end, He who made us on earth.

The Wedding of

Sir Gawain

and

Dame Ragnell

Introduction

"The Wedding of Sir Gawain and Dame Ragnell"
is one of the great stories in Middle English. Dame
Ragnell herself dominates it. She is first of all clever. She
frustrates her brother (though forgives him), saves King
Arthur, overcomes her enchantment, and marries Sir
Gawain, the great lover of the Round Table. The fact
that she is the ugliest woman in the world does not
affect her pride. She rightfully insists she is a lady, "not
just dung," and she rides beside King Arthur at Carlisle
Castle, though he is ashamed of her. She will not be
persuaded by Queen Guenevere to marry early in the
morning, when the church will be empty, but she insists
on being married at noon at high mass, when everyone

will attend. This pride intensifies the irony that she, the ugliest woman in the world, will marry Sir Gawain.

Gawain, always the true vassal to King Arthur, agrees in spite of her appearance. At first he shows no husbandly affection. Dame Ragnell, in addition to her other virtues, has a sense of humor. Gawain decides to love her and finds she is beautiful. His sense of shock is perfectly conveyed in "Oh Jesus, what are you?" And he is not blaspheming. Her answer is completely understated: "Sir, I am your wife, surely. Why are you being so unnatural?"

Altogether she is an unforgettable character. Chaucer adapted this story without Sir Gawain for his Wife of Bath in the *Canterbury Tales*, but in the process Dame Ragnell lost her name, pride, and sense of humor. The story was adapted again by John Gower in the *Confessio Amantis.* Certainly, however, the version of the tale we have here deserves to be considered a masterpiece on its own.

For its dramatic effect the tale depends on Gawain's reputation as a lover, and for its resolution on Gawain's loyalty to Arthur. Arthur, however, knowingly breaks his word to Gromer Somer Joure not to tell anyone of his difficulty. The author makes no apology and Arthur suffers no ill effect for this breach of one of the fundamental tenets of the knightly code.

The books that Arthur and Gawain collect are a unique detail and illustrate the complete education that a knight underwent in the late Middle Ages. Good use is made of the books in the story as well. When Arthur keeps his rendezvous with Gromer, he knows he has received the right answer from Dame Ragnell, but he lets Gromer think Gromer has won, first offering him the books to peruse. Then when Arthur tells Gromer the answer he received, Arthur stretches out the answer interminably.

Gromer Somer Joure's name can be translated, if not satisfactorily explained. "Gromer" is cognate to the Old Norse *gromr* and Middle English *grom*, an infant, boy, youth, servant. *Somer Joure* suggests "summer day" in English and French, but where this combination of three languages came from or why, we do not know.

This tale ends sadly. Gawain has his beautiful wife only five years, but as the story intimates, knighthood and marriage do not mix. Like so many other great works of medieval literature, "The Wedding of Sir Gawain and Dame Ragnell" has survived in a single manuscript, Rawlinson C 86, now in the Bodleian Library, Oxford. This manuscript contains a plea for the author of this story, who is in jail. This fact is all we know about this artist, that his pains are severe, a sad biography for one who wrote so fine a story.

The dialect of the original is that of the East Midlands of the late fifteenth century and with "An Adventure of Sir Gawain" is the only tale not preserved in a dialect of the north-west of England or Scotland. The stanzas are twelve lines in length.

> Lythe and listenythe the lif of a lord riche,
> The while that he lyvid was none hym liche,
> Nether in bowre ne in halle.
> In the tyme of Arthoure thys adventure betyd,
> And of the greatt adventure that he hym self
>   dyd,
> That kyng curteys and royalle.
> Of alle kynges Arture berythe the flowyr,
> And of alle knyghtod he bare away the honour,
> Where soeuere he wentt.
> In his contrey was nothyng butt chyvalry,
> And knyghtes were belovid [by] that doughty,
> For cowardes were eueremore shent.

The Tale

Listen and hear the life of a great lord who, while he lived, had no equal in cottage or in castle. This event took place in the time of Arthur, that King, courtly and royal, and is about one of his great adventures. Wherever he went, of all kings, Arthur bears the flower; of all knights, he bears the honor. The whole country was chivalrous in those days. All knights were valiant, and cowards were forever disgraced.

159

While you listen I shall tell you about King Arthur, how once he was hunting in Inglewood with all his bold knights. Now hear how this adventure happened. The King was sitting at his hunting station with his bow waiting to slay a wild deer; some of his lords were beside him. The King was aware that a great and beautiful hart was moving toward him, but in the underbrush the hart heard the hounds and stayed completely hidden.

"Everyone hold still!" said the King knowing what was going on. "I will go myself, and stalk that buck, if I can." The King took his bow and like a woodsman stooped low stalking the deer. When he came near it, the deer leapt into another thicket and the King crept after him. King Arthur stalked the deer in this way for about a half mile all alone. Finally he let an arrow fly, and it hit the deer accurately and surely, such grace God sent him. The deer tumbled to the earth into the deep undergrowth and the King began to butcher it to prepare the meat. As he was going about this, an extraordinary man came up to him, completely armed, a knight strong and powerful, who spoke very seriously to him:

"We are well met, King Arthur. You have done me wrong for many years, but now I shall repay you, unhappily for you. I believe the days of your life are nearly over. You gave my lands wrongly to Sir Gawain. What do you say about that, King, here alone?"

"Sir knight, what is your name, if you please?"

"Sir King," he replied, "Gromer Somer Joure, I tell you truly."

"If you are thinking of slaying me here, Sir Gromer Somer, you will get no honor from that. It seems to me you are a knight, but if you kill me unarmed, all knights will refuse you everywhere, and you will never be able to escape your shame. Give up this idea and listen to reason. Whatever is amiss, I shall amend it as you want before I go from here."

"No," said Sir Gromer Somer, "by Heaven's King, you shall not escape, indeed, for now I know I have the advantage over you. If I should let you go with only a few mocking words, another time you would defy me. I am not going to let that happen."

"Now," said the King, "so may God save me, spare my life and whatever you wish, I shall grant it you. You shall only be defamed to have slain me while hunting, you armed and I only in forest green, by God."

"All these arguments are not going to help you any, for I wish neither gold nor land. But you will promise to meet me on a certain day that I shall set, and in this same array."

"Yes," said the King, "here is my hand."

"True, but wait a minute, King, and hear me. First, you shall swear on my bright sword to tell me, when you arrive here, what it is that women love best, whether they are country girls or city girls. You shall meet me here personally, this day twelfth month. And you shall swear on my good sword that none of your knights shall come with you, by the Cross, neither friend nor foe. But if you do not bring an answer, no question but you shall lose your head for the effort. This is what you are going to have to swear to. What do you say now, King? Let's see! Let's finish this business."

"Sir, I grant you this. Now let me be gone. Although this is distasteful to me, I promise you, as I am a true king, to come again here at the end of twelve months and bring an answer to you."

"All right. Now go on your way, King Arthur. Your life is in my hand, I am sure. You are not even aware of the unhappiness you shall have. But now wait a minute, King Arthur. Don't try to trick me today, and you had better keep all this close to yourself. For I know, by Mary mild, if you betray me, your life is the first thing you will lose."

"Don't worry about my betraying you," said King Arthur. "That will never be. You will never find me an untrue knight. I would rather die. So farewell, sir knight, ill luck that we met, but I will come and still be alive on the day set, though I should never escape the consequences." Then the King blew his bugle that every knight heard and knew. They all quickly came to him, and they found the King and his deer, but he was melancholy and sad. That they did not like.

"Let us go home to Carlisle now," said King Arthur. "I do not enjoy hunting any more." By the way he looked, all the lords recognized that something had greatly disturbed him. They went on to Carlisle, but no one knew of his deep concern. His heart was heavy, and this heaviness lasted for so long a time that the knights worried about it markedly. At last Sir Gawain came to the King and said:

"Sir, I have been wondering seriously what has made you so sorrowful."

"I shall tell you, good Gawain," the King answered. "I was in the forest one day when I met an armed knight, and he told me something, but charged me I should not betray him. Therefore, I have to keep what he said secret, or else break my oath."

"No, do not fear, my lord, by gentle Mary. I am not a man who would dishonor you at any time."

"In truth I was hunting in Inglewood. You know that I slew a hart there by myself. There I met an armed knight who told me his name was Sir Gromer Somer Joure. I am worried about what happened with him." And Arthur told Gawain the story. When he had finished, Gawain said:

"Sir, cheer up. Let us make your horse ready and

ride off into far-away lands, and everywhere we meet either men or women, in faith you will ask them what they think women most desire. I shall ride another way and inquire of every man and woman the same way. I shall get as many answers as I can, and I shall write them in a book."

"We will do that," said the King immediately. "It is good advice, Gawain, by the Cross."

Soon both Sir Gawain and the King were ready. The King rode one way and Gawain the other, and they inquired of man and woman what it was that women most desired. Some said they loved to be well dressed, some said they loved to be flattered, some said they loved a lusty man who, in their arms, could kiss and make love to them. In short, some said one thing, some another. In this way Gawain recorded numerous answers, and when he had received as many as he could, so many it made a huge book for him, he came to the court again. The King arrived later with his book, and each examined the other's pages.

"We cannot fail this way," said Gawain.

"By God, I am still afraid," said the King. "I am going to Inglewood Forest and inquire some more. There is only a month until the day I agreed to, and I still may happen on some good ideas. Right now I think that is the best plan."

"Do as you wish," said Gawain. "Whatever you do, I agree to it willingly. Have no doubts, my lord, you will succeed. At least some of the answers will help you when you need them. Otherwise it would be bad luck indeed."

King Arthur rode into Inglewood Forest wherever a path took him. Along one of them he met a lady carrying a lute over her back, as ugly a creature as anyone ever saw. Her face was red, her nose snotted, her mouth wide, her teeth yellow, her eye rheumy, her teeth hung over her lips, and her cheeks were as fat as a woman's hips. Her neck was long and thick, her hair clotted and snarled. Her shoulders were a yard broad, and her breasts were a load for a strong horse. She was formed like a barrel. No tongue can adequately describe how foul she was, but she was ugly enough, and Arthur was dumbfounded.

She sat on a palfrey that was beautifully decorated, however, the harness set with gold and precious stones. It was extraordinary that so ugly a creature rode on so beautiful a mount. There seemed to be no reason for it. She rode up to Arthur and spoke.

"May God prosper you, Sir King. I am pleased that I have met with you. Speak with me, I advise you, before you go on, for your life is in my hands, let me warn you. You will find that out, if I do not prevent your losing it."

"Why, what do you want with me?" he asked.

"Sir, I would be happy now to talk with you and give you some good news. For of all the answers that you can boast about collecting, not any of them will help you, as you shall discover, by the Cross. You believe I do not know what you are thinking. But I warn you, I know every detail of it, and if I do not help you, you are dead. So allow me one thing, Sir King, and I will guarantee your life. Otherwise you will lose your head."

"What do you mean, lady? Tell me quickly. For I am suspicious of what you are saying. I do not think I need you. What do you want, fair lady? Let me know what you are talking about and why my life is in your hands. If you tell me, I will guarantee all you ask."

"If the truth were known, I am not just dung. You must grant me a knight as my husband. His name is Sir Gawain. And, if because of my answer your life is saved, I will make this agreement with you. Otherwise, just ignore what I wish. But if my answer saves your life, grant me Sir Gawain as my husband. Let me advise you now, Sir King, it has to be this way, or you are dead. Choose now, or soon you will lose your head. Tell me quickly."

"Mary," said the King, "I cannot promise you Sir Gawain as a husband. That depends only on him. But if what you say is true, then in addition to saving my life, I will do my utmost to make the wedding come about."

"Well," said she, "now go home again and speak convincingly to Sir Gawain, for I can save your life. Even though I am ugly, yet I am full of life, and through me, he can save your life or insure your death."

"Alas," said the King, "now I am truly unhappy that I should force Gawain to wed you. I will tell Gawain my troubles, and he will be loath to refuse. So ugly a woman as you are I never saw during my life in all the world. I do not know what I can do."

"No matter, Sir King. Though I am foul, even an owl can choose a mate. You will not get any more out of me. When you come again for your answer, I shall meet you right here in this place, or else I know you are lost."

"Now farewell, lady," said the King.

"Yes, sir," she said. "Men may think I look like an owl, yet I am a lady."

"What is your name, I pray you tell me."

"Sir King, I am called Dame Ragnell; in truth I never yet fooled a man."

"Dame Ragnell, now have a good day."

"Sir King, God speed you on your way. I will meet you right here." Thus they departed agreeably, and the King soon came back to Carlisle. His heart was heavy, and the first man he met was Sir Gawain who asked him:

"Have you had any success?"

"In truth," the King replied, "never as ill as this. Alas, I am on the point of losing my life."

"This cannot be," said Gawain. "I would rather be dead myself. This is bad news indeed."

"Gawain, today I met the ugliest woman that I ever saw. She said she would save my life, but first she would have you as her husband. This is the reason I am woe begone and my heart is heavy."

"Is that all?" Gawain asked. "I shall wed her and wed her again even if she is a fiend and as foul as Beelzebub. By the Cross, I will wed her or no longer count me as a friend, for you are my king and you have honored me in many a battle. Therefore I shall not refuse. It is my obligation to save your life, my lord, or else I were false to you and a great coward. And in this way my honor is increased."

"Many thanks, Gawain," Arthur said. "Of all the knights that I have ever known, you bear the flower. My honor and my life you save forever, and therefore you will never lose my love, on my word as King of this land."

Within five or six days the King had to go his way for his answer, so he and Sir Gawain rode out of town alone, no one else with them. When they were within the forest, the King said:

"Sir Gawain, farewell. I must go west. You can go no further."

"God speed you on your journey. I wish I could go with you, for I am sad at having to depart." After leaving Gawain, the King had ridden on a little more than a mile when he met Dame Ragnell.

"Ah, Sir King, you are welcome here. I know you bring Gawain's promise with you."

"Now," said the King, "since it won't be any other way, tell me your own answer and save my life. Gawain shall wed you. He has promised me this to save my life, and you shall have your desire both at home and in bed. Therefore tell me the answer to my question immediately."

"Sir," replied Dame Ragnell, "now you shall know what all women, high class or low, desire most, and I am not going to vary the truth. Some people say we want to be beautiful; some say we want to keep company with many different men, or that we want to have passion in bed, or we want to marry often. But you people really don't know. We desire something else. You men say women want to be considered not old but fresh and young so with flattery and wit and caresses you can have what you want from us. That idea is pretty good, I can't lie about that.

"But now you shall know. We desire above everything else to have power over men, both high and low. When we have power, everything else is ours, even though a knight may be the most fierce of all and always wins the tourneys. Our desire is to have sovereignty over the most manly of men. This is the end of all our skill and learning. There, Sir King, go your way and tell that knight as I have told you, that this is what we desire most. He will be angry and cranky and curse the woman who taught you, for all his effort is lost. Go now, King, and keep your promise, for your life is now safe, I dare say."

The King rode out a great way as fast as he could, through mire, moor, and fen to the place where he met Sir Gromer. Sir Gromer spoke to the King sternly:

"Come on now, Sir King, let us see what your answer will be, for I am all ready." The King pulled out his two books.

"Sir, here is my answer, I say. For at least some of these answers must help me." Sir Gromer looked at each one of them.

"No, no, Sir King. You are a dead man. Now you shall bleed."

"Wait a minute, Sir Gromer," said King Arthur, "I have one more answer that shall make everything sure."

"Let's see," Sir Gromer then said, "or else, as help me God, you shall have your death as your pay, I tell you surely."

"Now," said the King, "I see, as I suppose, there is little gentility in you, by God who helps us. Here is our answer, that all women, both free women and those in bondage, I say no more, but above all else, women most desire power, for that is their pleasure and their greatest wish. To have the rule of the manliest man, then are they happy, and thus they gave me the knowledge to rule you, Gromer, sir."

"And she who told you now, Sir Arthur, I pray God to see her burn in fire, for that was my sister, Dame Ragnell, that old Scot. May God shame her. Otherwise I would have tamed you. Now all my effort is for nothing. Go where you want, King Arthur, for you no longer need to worry about me. Alas that I ever saw this day. Now I know that you will be my enemy, and that is a sad song for me. The words of my music shall be, 'Farewell forever.'"

"No," said the King, "and that I guarantee. You shall never find me in such a plight as this again, and if you do, I deserve to be bound and beaten. I have armor for my defense that I promised to God. That you may well believe."

"Now have a good day," said Sir Gromer.

"Farewell," said Sir Arthur, "and I am glad I was successful, and may I continue to prosper so." King Arthur turned his horse into the plain and soon met Dame Ragnell again.

"Sir King, I am glad you have been successful," she said. "I told you that you would be in every way. Now you must hold to your promise. Since I alone have saved your life, Gawain, the noble knight, must marry me, Sir Arthur."

"Lady, I promise you I shall not fail in my promise.

If you will be governed by my counsel, you will get what you wish."

"Now do not try any tricks, Sir King. I won't have it. I shall be married and in public, before I leave you. Or you will be shamed. Ride ahead and I will come after into your court, Sir King Arthur. I do not want to shame anyone. Remember how I saved your life, so do not quarrel with me now. If you do, the blame will be on you."

As they rode along, the King was ashamed of her, but she, ignoring his embarrassment, just rode along until they came to Carlisle. When they went into the castle, she rode right beside him, and for no one would she change her position. The King was not pleased about this, and wondered where such a foul, horrible creature came from. The people of the court had never seen so ugly a person.

"Arthur, King, fetch me Sir Gawain," she said when they entered the great hall, "in the presence of these knights and quickly. That I may now be certain of your promise. In sickness and in health we will pledge our troth together before all your chivalry. This is your promise; let's see it done. Bring on Sir Gawain, my love, right now. Do not keep me waiting." Then Gawain came out.

"Sir, I am ready to fulfill my pledges as I promised you," he said.

"God have mercy," said Dame Ragnell, "for your sake I wish I were a beautiful woman, for you have such good will." Then Sir Gawain plighted his troth to her in sickness and in health as he was a true knight, and Dame Ragnell was happy.

"Alas, poor Sir Gawain," said Dame Guenevere, and the ladies in her chamber repeated what she said and wept for the knight.

"Alas," repeated both the King and his knights, sad

that Gawain should have to marry such a person, so foul and horrible. She had only two teeth like boar tusks the length of a hand on two sides of her mouth. One tusk went up and the other down. Her mouth was enormously wide and was surrounded with many gray hairs. Her lips hung over her chin.

In spite of her appearance she would not be married in any way but with a public announcement in all the shires, both in the towns and in the boroughs. All the ladies in the country cried when they learned the marriage would take place. On the day the foul lady was to marry Sir Gawain, all the ladies pitied him, and the Queen asked Dame Ragnell earnestly that she be married early in the morning.

"As secretly as possible," she requested.

"Not at all," Dame Ragnell answered. "By Heaven's King, I will not do that for all the world. In spite of anything you may say, I want to be married quite openly. I made that agreement with the King. Let me relieve you of any doubt. I will not go to church until the time of high mass, and afterward I will dine in the great hall in the midst of all the court."

"I am agreed," said Dame Guenevere, "but it seems to me more honorable for you to be married quietly."

"As for that, my lady, God save you, this day I will still have my honor, and I say it without boasting."

She made ready to go to the church, and all the people agreed she was dressed so richly that her clothes would have taken any prize. She was arrayed more attractively than Dame Guenevere without exaggeration. Her clothes were worth three thousand marks of sound gold nobles. But of the woman herself, such foulness I never heard tell. To make a long story short, so foul a sow no man ever saw.

And as soon as she was married, the people all hurried to the castle and to the banquet. Many people boast of a rich banquet, but you can believe that at this banquet there was more than enough, both of domestic food and wild meat. In King Arthur's court there was never any lack of what could be acquired by the hand of man either in the forest or in the pasture. And minstrels arrived from a far-away land.

That horrible woman was mistress of the high dais, but she was crude and ill mannered in every way. When the service came before her, she ate as much as any six who were there. Her nails were three inches long and she tore her food apart with them, eating all by herself. She finished three capons, three curlews, several huge baked dishes, by God. All the guests remarked that nothing was put in front of her but she gobbled every scrap of it, that horrible damsel. She continued eating right to the finish of the meal until the servants took the tablecloth away and all the guests had washed, as is customary. Every knight and squire cursed that the devil might gnaw her bones.

When the banquet was over, Gawain and Dame Ragnell left the hall and went to their chamber.

"Ah, Sir Gawain," Dame Ragnell said, "since I have married you, now show me your courtesy in bed. This right cannot be denied. Truly, if I were beautiful, you would have acted differently. You would not have bothered to worry if we were married or not. So, for Arthur's sake, at least give me a kiss. I ask you to do this, anyway. Let us see how well you kiss."

"I will do more than kiss you," Gawain said, "and before God." He turned toward her and saw beside him the most beautiful woman he had ever imagined with no exceptions.

"Now, what is your will?" she said quietly.

"Oh Jesus," he said, "what are you?"

"I am your wife, surely. Why are you being so unnatural?"

"Oh, my lady, I am to blame. I ask for mercy, fair madame—I did not imagine. Now you are certainly a beautiful woman, and even today you were the ugliest person I ever saw. I am certainly fortunate to have you change this way." He took her in his arms and kissed her with great passion.

"Sir," she said, "you may have me beautiful. But you must choose, may God save you, for my beauty is not constant. You may have me beautiful at night for yourself alone and ugly during the day for all other men, or at night ugly for yourself, and in the day beautiful for others. You have to choose one or the other. Choose one, sir knight, whichever you prefer."

"Alas," said Sir Gawain, "the choice is hard. To choose what is best is difficult. To have you fair at night and no more would grieve me deeply, for I would lose my honor and respect. To have you fair during the day but ugly at night, then I would lose my pleasure. Although I would be glad to choose best, still I do not know what in the world I can say. So do as you wish, my lady dear. The choice I put in your hands. Do with me as you wish, for I am bound to you. I give the choice to you. Both my body and my goods, my heart and all parts of me are all yours, to buy and sell—that I swear to God."

"Many thanks, courteous knight," said the lady. "Of all the knights in the world you must be the most blessed, for now you honor me. You shall have me beautiful both day and night, and I will be fair and attractive as long as I live. Therefore do not worry, for my stepmother transformed me by an enchantment, may God have mercy on her. I would have been transformed until the best man in England married me and gave me sovereignty over his body and his goods. I was deformed until that happened. And you, sir knight, courteous Gawain, have given me sovereignty, certainly. You will not ever be sorry about that. Now kiss me, sir knight, right here, I pray you. Be happy and enjoy yourself, for it has turned out well for both of us."

There they had joy unimaginable as was right and natural, both of them alone. Both she and Sir Gawain thanked God and Mary mild that she recovered from her enchantment. They had all kinds of pleasure in their chamber and thanked our Saviour for it. I can tell you truthfully, they stayed awake until dawn with their joy and play, and then the beautiful girl wanted to arise.

"You shall not," said Sir Gawain. "We will lie and sleep late this morning, and then let the King call us to dine."

"I'd like that," said the girl, and so the time passed until midday.

"Sirs," said the King to his nobles, "let us go and see if Sir Gawain is still alive. I am much afraid that the devil might have killed him. I have to find out. Let us go and see what has happened." All of them came to the chamber door. "Get up!" called the King to Sir Gawain, "why do you sleep so long in bed?"

"Mary," said Sir Gawain, "Sir King, surely, I would be glad if you would let me be, for I am contented. Wait a minute, I will open the door. I believe you will say that I have been fortunate, and you will know why I am reluctant to get up." Sir Gawain arose, and took his lovely bride by the hand over to the door and opened it. She was standing in her smock by the fire. Her hair down to her knees was a red gold filigree.

"She is my pleasure," Gawain said to Arthur. "Sir, this is my wife, Dame Ragnell, who saved your life." And he told the King and the Queen how suddenly her transformation was accomplished and why she had once been ugly.

"I thank God," said the Queen. "I thought, Sir Gawain, she wanted to do you harm, and in my heart I was afraid. But obviously, I can see the contrary here."

There was pleasure, revel, and enjoyment, and every one said she was a beautiful woman. The King told all of them how Dame Ragnell had saved his life.

"Or my death had been assured," he said. "She saved me from death for the love of Sir Gawain." And Dame Ragnell told the King what choice and what power Gawain had given her.

"May God thank him for his courtesy," she said. "He saved me from ill fortune and a degradation that was foul and grim. Therefore, courteous knight and noble Gawain, I shall certainly never anger you. I make that promise here. And I will be obedient all the days of my life, and to God above, I guarantee never to argue with you."

"Thank you very much," Gawain then said, "I am well contented with you, and I know I always will be. She shall have my love," Gawain told them all, "and she will not need for anything, for she has been so kind to me."

"She is the most beautiful woman now in the castle," the Queen said. "I swear by St. John. You shall always have my love, because you saved my lord, Arthur, on my word as a gentlewoman."

She and Gawain were the parents of Guinglain, who was a strong knight and a member of the Round Table. At every feast day Dame Ragnell was always the most beautiful wherever she was, and Gawain loved her very much. In all his life he never loved anyone as well, and I can tell you truthfully that willingly he lay beside her both day and night.

He did not joust as he had, and Arthur wondered

about this. Dame Ragnell asked the King to be a good
lord to Sir Gromer.

"Even though he offended you," she said.

"Yes, lady, I shall do that now for your sake, for I
know he will never make amends for the unkindness he
did to me."

Now to make this long story short, I will bring it
soon to a close. This noble lady lived only for five years,
and Gawain mourned for her all his life, I can tell you
truly. In her whole life she never made him unhappy,
and no woman was ever dearer to him. My tale ends
here. She was the fairest lady in all England when she
was alive, I understand. So Arthur the King said.

So the adventure of King Arthur ends, who often in
his days was sorely grieved, and so ends the wedding
of Gawain. Gawain was often wedded during his lifetime, but he never loved a woman as well, as I have
heard people say. This adventure occurred in Ingles-
wood as good King Arthur went hunting, as people
have said.

Now God, as Thou was born in Bethlehem, never
allow their souls to burn in the fire of Hell. And Jesus,
as Thou was born of a virgin, help him out of his sorrows
who wrote this story, for he is in the hands of many
jailers who keep him securely with torture wrong and
awful. Now God, as Thou art the true royal King, help
him out of danger who wrote this story, for he has been
in danger for a long time. And give thy servant pity, and
I yield my body and soul into Thy hand, because his
pains are severe. Here ends the wedding of Sir Gawain
and Dame Ragnell, because she helped King Arthur.

Notes

General Introduction

[1]Gwyn Jones and Thomas Jones, trans. *Mabinogion* (London: J. M. Dent, 1949), p. 108.

[2]William of Malmesbury, *De gestis regum Anglorum,* ed. William Stubbs (London: H. M. Stationery Office, 1887-89). II, 342.

[3]B.J. Whiting, "Gawain: His Reputation, His Courtesy, and His Appearance in Chaucer's Squire's Tale," *Mediaeval Studies* 9 (1947), 221.

Sir Gawain and the Carl of Carlisle

[1]Gwyn Jones and Thomas Jones, trans., *Mabinogion* (London: J. M. Dent, 1949), p. 107.

[2]Ibid., p. 106.

Bibliography

General Introduction

Arthurian Literature in the Middle Ages, ed. R. S. Loomis. Oxford: Clarendon, 1959.

Arthur King of Britain, ed. Richard L. Brengle. New York: Appleton-Century-Crofts, 1964.

Baugh, Albert C. "The Middle English Romance: Some Questions of Creation, Presentation, and Preservation," *Speculum* 42 (1967), 1–31.

Delort, Robert. *Life in the Middle Ages*, trans. Robert Allen. New York: Universe Books, 1973.

Erikson, Erik. "Youth: Fidelity and Diversity." *The Challenge of Youth*, ed. E. H. Erikson. New York: Doubleday, 1965.

Geoffrey of Monmouth. *Histories of the Kings of Britain*, trans. Sebastian Evans. London: J. M. Dent, 1941.

Loomis, Roger Sherman. *The Development of Arthurian Romance*. New York: Harper, 1963.

Malory, Sir Thomas. *The Works of Sir Thomas Malory*, ed. Eugene Vinaver. Oxford University Press, 1965.

Robinson, Edwin Arlington. *Collected Poems: Merlin, Lancelot, Tristram*. New York: Macmillan, 1927.

Syr Gawayne: A Collection of Ancient Romance-poems by Scotish and English Authors, ed. Sir Frederic Madden. Edinburgh: Bannatyne Club, 1839.

Tennyson, Alfred. *Idylls of the King*, ed. W. J. Rolfe. Boston: Houghton Mifflin, 1896.

179

Weston, Jessie L. *The Legend of Sir Gawain.* London: Nutt, 1897.

Whiting, B. J. "Gawain: His Reputation, His Courtesy, and His Appearance in Chaucer's Squire's Tale," *Mediaeval Studies* 9 (1947), 189–234.

Sir Gawain and the Carl of Carlisle

Ackerman, Robert W. "The Carl of Carlisle." *Arthurian Literature in the Middle Ages,* ed. R. S. Loomis. Oxford: Clarendon, 1959. Pp. 493–95.

Sir Gawain and the Carl of Carlisle in Two Versions, ed. Auvo Kurvinen. Helsinki, 1951.

Syre Gawene and the Carle of Carelyle, ed. R. W. Ackerman. No. 8 of *Contributions in Modern Philology.* Ann Arbor, Mich.: University of Michigan Press, 1947.

The Green Knight

Ackerman, Robert W. "The Green Knight," in *Arthurian Literature in the Middle Ages,* ed. R. S. Loomis. Oxford: Clarendon, 1959. Pp. 497–98.

Arthurian Chronicles Represented by Wace and Layamon, ed. and trans. Eugene Mason. London: J. M. Dent, 1912. Pp. 209–11.

Kittredge, G. L. *A Study of Gawain and the Green Knight.* Cambridge, Mass.: Harvard University Press, 1916. Pp. 125–36, 282 –89.

The Percy Folio Manuscript, eds. J. W. Hales and F. J. Furnivall. London: Trubner, 1967–68. II, 58–77.

Sir Gawain and the Green Knight, ed. Sir I. Gollancz, red. M. Day and M. S. Serjeantson. London: Early English Text Society, 1940. P. xxix.

Sir Gawain and the Green Knight, ed. J. R. R. Tolkien and E. V. Gordon, rev. Norman Davis. Oxford: Clarendon, 1967. Pp. xiv-xv.

The Adventures at Tarn Wadling

"The Awntyrs off Arthure at the Terne Wathelyne," ed. F. J. Amours. *Scottish Alliterative Poems in Riming Stanzas.* Edinburgh: Scottish Text Society, 1897. Pp. 116–171.

"The Awntyrs off Arthure at the Terne Wathelyne," ed. R. J. Gates. Philadelphia: University of Pennsylvania Press, 1969.

Klausner, David N. "Exempla and The Awntyrs of Arthure," *Medieval Studies* 34 (1972), 307–25.

Matthews, William. *The Tragedy of Arthur.* Berkeley: University of California Press, 1960.

O'Loughlin, J. L. N. "The English Alliterative Romance." *Arthurian Literature in the Middle Ages,* ed. R. S. Loomis. Oxford: Clarendon, 1959. Pp. 526–27.

Golagros and Gawain

"The Knightly Tale of Golagros and Gawane." Amours, F. J., ed. *Scottish Alliterative Poems in Riming Stanzas.* Edinburgh: Scottish Text Society, 1897. Pp. 1–46.

Ketrick, P. J., *Relation of Golagros and Gawane to the Old French Perceval.* Washington: Catholic University Press, 1931.

An Adventure of Sir Gawain

Ackerman, Robert W. "The Gest of Sir Gawain." *Arthurian Literature in the Middle Ages,* ed. R. S. Loomis. Oxford: Clarendon, 1950. Pp. 500–501.

Bennett, R. E. "Sources of 'The Jeaste of Syr Gawayne.'" *Journal of English and Germanic Philology* 33 (1934), 57–63.

The Avowing of King Arthur, Sir Gawain, Sir Kay, and Baldwin of Britain

Ackerman, Robert W. "The Avowing of King Arthur, Sir Gawain, Sir Kay, and Baldwin of Britain." *Arthurian Literature in the Middle Ages,* ed. R. S. Loomis. Oxford: Clarendon, 1959. Pp. 499–500.

The Avowing of King Arthur, Sir Gawain, Sir Kay, and Baldwin of Britain, ed. Christopher Brookhouse. *Anglistica* 15 (1968), 60–96.

The Avowing of King Arthur, Sir Gawain, Sir Kay, and Baldwin of Britain, ed. W. H. French and C. B. Hale. *Middle English Metrical Romances.* New York: Prentice-Hall, 1930. Pp. 605–46.

Greenlaw, Edwin A. "The Vows of Baldwin." *PMLA* 21 (1906), 575–636.

The Wedding of Sir Gawain and Dame Ragnell

Ackerman, Robert W., " 'The Wedding of Sir Gawain and Dame Ragnell' and Chaucer's 'Wife of Bath's Tale.' " *Arthurian Literature in the Middle Ages,* ed. R. S. Loomis. Oxford: Clarendon, 1959. Pp. 501–505.

The Weddynge of Sir Gawene and Dame Ragnell, ed. Laura Sumner. *Smith College Studies in Modern Languages* 5 (1923).

"The Weddynge of Sir Gawene and Dame Ragnell," ed. B. J. Whiting. *Sources and Analogues of Chaucer's Canterbury Tales,* ed. W. F. Bryan and Germaine Dempster. New Yourk: Humanities, 1958. Pp. 242–64.

Index